What's Wrong with Money?

What's Wrong with Money?

The Biggest Bubble of All

MICHAEL ASHTON

WILEY

Published by John Wiley & Sons, Inc., Hoboken, New Jersey.
Published simultaneously in Canada.

For general information on our other products and services or for technical support, please contact our Customer Care Department within the United States at (800) 762-2974, outside the United States at (317) 572-3993 or fax (317) 572-4002.

Wiley publishes in a variety of print and electronic formats and by print-on-demand. Some material included with standard print versions of this book may not be included in e-books or in print-on-demand. If this book refers to media such as a CD or DVD that is not included in the version you purchased, you may download this material at http://booksupport.wiley.com. For more information about Wiley products, visit www.wiley.com.

Library of Congress Cataloging-in-Publication Data:

ISBN 9781119191018 (Hardcover)
ISBN 9781119191179 (ePDF)
ISBN 9781119191162 (ePub)

Cover Images: Soap bubble © rusm/iStockphoto;
US one hundred dollar bill © burakpekakcan/iStockphoto;
Pushpin © rimglow/iStockphoto
Cover Design: Wiley

Printed in the United States of America
10 9 8 7 6 5 4 3 2 1

This book is dedicated to my wife, Diane, and to our joint investments in the future: Andy and Lila.

Contents

Preface

Every person in authority, whether at the Federal Reserve (Fed) or the European Central Bank (ECB), in the White House or at 10 Downing Street, on Capitol Hill or in Parliament, says that we should not worry. Sure, there are holdouts—people who worry, like we do—but they are marginalized as cranks or backbenchers.

What are we worried about? In 2000, we had a bursting stock market bubble that produced a fairly brief but painful recession. Central banks and legislators sprang into action by drastically cutting interest rates and extending jobless benefits, among other things. "Don't worry! It's Greenspan to the rescue!" we were told. For a while, it seemed as if they were right. The economy recovered, although we now realize that the actions of the authorities set up another, bigger bubble.

In 2007, the second bubble within a single decade started to come undone; it popped in 2008. The ensuing recession was deeper, and longer, and the response from monetary and fiscal authorities was more dramatic. The scale of the response was an order of magnitude larger, with trillions of dollars of deficit spending and the implementation of quantitative easing (QE) on a massive scale. The breadth of the response was also impressive, with every major central bank not only dropping interest rates but also implementing its own version of QE. Dramatic? The response was desperate. Certain central banks pursued policies that drew criticism at the time, not because they were of limited effectiveness but because they were of questionable legality under the central bank's authorizing legislation. But it was a classic case of the ends being taken to justify the means: In the end, the world was saved from financial immolation and if you have to break a few eggs to make an omelet, who cares? After the fact, even some of the original critics begrudgingly recanted, saying that in the heat of the moment clearly something had to be done, and any alternative proposal would have to be tested against a policy that, ultimately, worked.

In the United States, the unemployment rate is below 6 percent again. Banks are lending. The hyperinflation predicted by the hyperventilated never, in fact, happened. Budget deficits are coming back down. Japan and the Eurozone have seemingly averted deflationary collapses as well, and although many bank depositors in Cyprus were "bailed in" (in other words, their money on deposit was confiscated), the European currency union has so far proven inviolate. Although, to be fair, we haven't heard the last of Greece.

Winning!

So why are we worried? The crisis is over! Disaster averted. And soon—although we have to use our imagination about what "soon" is—the Federal Reserve will begin increasing interest rates to put monetary policy on a more normal footing. All of the worst predictions have failed to materialize. Game, set, and match to the financial interventionists. Right?

We are worried because this doesn't feel right. We see a perpetual motion machine, and although we can't write down the physics equations for why it shouldn't be working, we have intuition that tells us it shouldn't. If the seemingly insane scope and scale of the policy response was successful in doing what it is purported to have done—to have added millions of jobs, saved thousands of banks and put the stock market on the moon—with no evident side effects, then why the heck haven't central banks and legislatures been doing this forever? Eat all the chocolate you want, and don't gain weight! It sounds like a great deal.

But we know something is amiss. This book describes what that is. The unfortunate fact is that each subsequent crisis has only been repaired by weakening a more fundamental layer of our financial lives. The crumbling equity market edifice was repaired, at the cost of the housing and credit markets. The housing and credit markets have been repaired, but at what cost?

This book is about the most fundamental layer of all: the structure of money itself. Over the last century, our concept of what money is, at its very root, has gradually changed. What backs money today is simply this: trust. There is nothing else behind our dollars, our euros, our sterling, our yen, our francs ... but trust that someone else will accept it at a reasonably predictable level in exchange for stuff we need. And this is why it matters so much that policymaker responses to the last few crises have whittled away at that trust. This is why it is so disturbing that these policymakers say "trust us" while they monkey with money.

Never before has so much ridden on trust. And never before has that trust been so abused, and so stretched. What's wrong with money? Nothing, and everything.

What's Wrong with Money: The Biggest Bubble of All is structured thus:

In Part I of the book I explain what money is, how it differs from related concepts of wealth and currency, and why we need money in the first place. How has money evolved from being backed by something to being backed by only trust? What is *fiat* money, and why is it any better or worse than non-fiat types? What can we learn from the experience of bitcoin? One of the things we can learn from history is how fiat money regimes tend to end. Perhaps that will help us figure out where we are going.

In Part II, I tackle the current circumstance. It is key to understand how the actions of fiscal and monetary agents in response to the global credit crisis have impacted us today, and how those actions narrow the set of potential future outcomes. And I will tell you how I personally think this whole episode is likely to end. Spoiler alert: There is no perpetual motion machine.

In Part III, I tell you how this should affect the way you arrange your investments, today.

Acknowledgments

I can't believe I wrote the whole thing.

This book was the surprising (to me) result of an inspiring conversation I had with my good friend Karl Strobl, who admonished me to warn the countryside about the perils of relying on a system of money whose edifice is built on the shifting sands of trust. From the moment that Karl suggested the title *What's Wrong with Money*, the book came alive in my head and in a few short months it was reality.

The whole team at Wiley is terrific, but I must single out Executive Editor Bill Falloon. Bill has rejected (kindly) so many of my ideas in the past that when he said he liked this one I knew that it must really be a good idea. Also special thanks to Meg Freeborn, who quarterbacked the project and was so encouraging throughout.

My wonderful family deserves special mention, and not simply because of their boundless love and support. I was tasked with this manuscript only a few days before we began a month-long road trip, complete with dog—and deadline. My family tolerated my sneaking away to write a thousand words here, a thousand words there, and never complained. Words cannot express my appreciation. A road trip with a dog is stressful enough already!

About the Author

Michael Ashton is managing principal at Enduring Investments LLC, an independently owned investment management company that offers focused inflation-market expertise.

Prior to founding Enduring Investments, Mr. Ashton worked as a trader, strategist, and salesman at some of the most prestigious financial institutions in the world, including Deutsche Bank, Bankers Trust, Barclays Capital, and J.P. Morgan.

Mr. Ashton is a pioneer in the U.S. inflation derivatives market, a proven innovator in inflation markets, and an outspoken advocate of the need to provide effective client inflation solutions that are unique, transparent, liquid, scalable, and inexpensive. While at Barclays, he traded the first interbank U.S. CPI swaps. He was a driving force in the creation of the CPI Futures contract that the Chicago Mercantile Exchange listed in February 2004 and was the lead market maker for that contract. Mr. Ashton has written extensively about the use of inflation-indexed products for hedging real exposures.

Mr. Ashton graduated summa cum laude with a BA in Economics (1990) from Trinity University in San Antonio, Texas. He earned his CFA designation in 2001. He is married with two children and lives in Morristown, New Jersey. This is his second book: *Maestro, My Ass!* was published in 2009.

PART I

How Money Lives and Dies

CHAPTER 1

What Is Money, and Why Do We Need It?

Stop for a minute and think about that dollar (or euro or yen) in your pocket or in your bank account. What does it mean? Before you read further, think about that question. What is the *significance* of saying, "I have a dollar"? What does a dollar represent?

The meaning of a dollar—and, henceforth, I will often use "dollar" for ease of exposition, but you understand that I mean *your currency unit*—is best understood by thinking of the two endpoints of the period of time during which I possess it.

I *receive* a dollar in exchange for something—very often, my labor. In fact, that is how most of us receive our dollars. In the United States (in 2015), about 51 percent of total personal income was received in the form of wages and salaries. Another 12 percent was in "employer contributions for employee pension and insurance funds" and "employer contributions for government social insurance," though to be honest neither of those sounds like the kind of income that puts dollars in my pocket today. (For those readers who are curious: 14 percent is from Social Security, Medicare, and Medicaid; 14 percent is from wages and dividends; the balance is from a variety of sources.)[1]

So the dollar in my pocket is most likely the result of my labor. And where does it go? About 42 percent goes to Girl

Scout cookies...wait, that's just me. Your answers here will vary, but the salient point is that those dollars are in our possession temporarily until they go to buy goods and services. For you, for your family, or for your heirs—ultimately, a dollar is just a placeholder for "what I will buy, someday."

That greenback is to your labor what a battery is to electricity: It holds the input (labor) in a form that is easy to hold, until it is ready to be used.

This is an important function for money, and you can see this by thinking about a primitive society that doesn't have money.

A Pre-Money Society

Consider Elmer the farmer. Elmer grows corn and raises chickens. This works for him because the chickens will eat surplus corn, so he has a decent diet of chicken, eggs, and corn. Nicely done, Elmer.

Elmer's neighbor, Margo, raises cows and wheat. This doesn't work *quite* as well as Elmer's setup, but the cows eat the chaff from the wheat and graze on her fallow acres, so Margo enjoys beef, milk, and bread. She, like Elmer, is also fairly self-sufficient.

Both Elmer and Margo can easily improve their positions. Elmer can offer three eggs in exchange for a quart of milk, for example, or swap chickens for cows. This is called a barter economy, and you can easily imagine how this economy can be enlarged with more of Margo's and Elmer's neighbors producing and trading vegetables, sheep, fish, and so on. This little commune could lead a bucolic existence, even without money. Consider, though, three potential problems with this setup.

First Problem: Slippery Standards of Exchange

What happens to this little vignette if Margo complains that Elmer always gives her the three *smallest* eggs in exchange for a quart of milk? In a barter economy, our two actors would resolve this issue by reaching some agreement on the size of the eggs that need to be exchanged for one quart of milk at a three-to-one ratio. The eggs must be just *so* big, but (for Elmer's protection) no larger than *this*. But what if Elmer has already traded all of his eggs of that size, and only has small eggs left? Moreover, *every* exchange of goods (or services! Margo's neighbor Olaf builds fences for food!) will have a set of standards to ensure a fair exchange. These standards may be established and maintained at a trading post or just developed organically (no pun intended) by the society, as a series of bilateral exchanges serves to establish not only the price but what we would call the *contract grade*;[2] but these details need to be agreed for each transaction.

Second Problem: Long-Term Storage

How does a system like this deal with a circumstance like Margo's Milk Miracle, the memorable year when Margo's cows doubled milk production for reasons no one ever figured out. (Was Margo's milking more aggressive? Was the grass that year especially lush? Who knows? Milk is mysterious.) Margo tried to trade away her milk by pre-paying this year's milk for next year's eggs. She had Olaf build fences to nowhere, threw milk parties, and so on. She would have liked to save some for next year, or put some toward her retirement (or for the retirement of Bessie, her bell cow); but in the end, a lot of the milk spoiled. Milk doesn't store well.

Third Problem: Different Trading Interests

Barter depends critically on an intersection of interests. If I have A and want B, and you have B and want A, then barter is feasible. But there is complexity when Margo needs a fence but Olaf—who is on a very restrictive gluten-free vegan diet—doesn't eat beef, milk, or wheat. How does Margo get her fence, if she has nothing to exchange for Olaf's services? Margo needs to do some additional work: Olaf needs a new fireplace, which the mason can provide. But Minnie the mason is lactose-intolerant and has all the beef and wheat she needs for the next month already laid in. However, Minnie needs shoes, which Carlos the cobbler can provide. Carlos needs leather, which Tessa the tanner has; Tessa, fortunately, can use a cow for not only beef but for the hide as well.[3] *So*, all that Margo needs to do is to give a cow to Tessa in exchange for leather; trade the leather to Carlos for shoes; swap the shoes to Minnie in exchange for a fireplace for Olaf; and then Olaf can build a fence for Margo. *If*, that is, one cow equals the right amount of leather to get the right number of pairs of shoes to persuade Minnie to build a fireplace. Building a fireplace is a lot of work, so Minnie might require *not only* shoes but also salsa, which Margo can get from Sadie the chef, who needs...

Maybe it would be easier to invent money. Money can resolve each of these problems and make the economic system of the whole community work more smoothly.

Money as a Unit of Account

You may have heard that money serves as a *unit of account*. This function is useful for solving the problem of slippery standards of exchange. If Elmer doesn't trade eggs for milk, but rather, eggs for money, which he then uses to buy milk, then we don't need a list of standards of exchanging eggs for milk, because Margo knows one unit of currency is worth three eggs of a certain size. We can adjust more easily for deviations from "contract grade" by, for example, paying more money for bigger eggs rather than having a whole different set of exchange prices for big eggs versus milk than for small eggs versus milk. This also greatly simplifies the price list. If we posted all of the prices at a trading post, the basic price list for only the 10 products I have mentioned so far would have 45 entries, and looks like Table 1.1.

If we introduce money as a unit of account, then the trading post price list has only 10 elements and reads like the somewhat smaller Table 1.2 (let a unit of currency be represented by the arbitrary symbol ⚹):

We can illustrate this same point by picturing all of the connections this way. In the following chart, each *price*—the rate of exchange of one good or service for another—is represented by a line. Figure 1.1 is a chart of the price interactions *without* money; Figure 1.2 is a chart *with* money.

Remember, this exercise was for only 10 goods. Imagine the difference in clutter if, instead, there are 50 or 100 things being exchanged in our little community! In fact, why imagine? Table 1.3 shows the difference in the number of connections, according to the number of goods, *without* money and *with* money.

You get the picture. Moving from a barter system to one based on money produces *tremendous* efficiency gains for the economy; for anything other than a very small economy, it is almost impossible to have an economy *without* money.

As an aside, this same exact principle is at work in myriad modern applications. If you are flying from Little Rock, Arkansas, to Des Moines, Iowa, you will almost certainly connect in one of a few large hubs such as DFW Airport, Chicago O'Hare, or Atlanta. It takes far fewer planes and vastly less fuel to move passengers through a hub-and-spoke system (such as is illustrated in the network diagram with money in Figure 1.2) than it does to transport them directly. In the same way, using money as the "hub" for an exchange of value makes economic

TABLE 1.1   Sample Price List for Trading Post in a Relatively Simple Barter Economy

3	eggs	=	1	quart(s) of milk
8	eggs	=	1	square yard(s) of leather
24	eggs	=	1	bushel(s) of wheat
36	eggs	=	1	bushel(s) of corn
40	eggs	=	1	pair of shoes
48	eggs	=	1	chicken(s)
240	eggs	=	1	fence (50 feet)
360	eggs	=	1	cow(s)
480	eggs	=	1	fireplace(s)
8	quart(s) of milk	=	3	square yard(s) of leather
8	quart(s) of milk	=	1	bushel(s) of wheat
12	quart(s) of milk	=	1	bushel(s) of corn
40	quart(s) of milk	=	3	pair of shoes
16	quart(s) of milk	=	1	chicken(s)
80	quart(s) of milk	=	1	fence (50 feet)
120	quart(s) of milk	=	1	cow(s)
160	quart(s) of milk	=	1	fireplace(s)
3	square yard(s) of leather	=	1	bushel(s) of wheat
9	square yard(s) of leather	=	2	bushel(s) of corn
5	square yard(s) of leather	=	1	pair of shoes
6	square yard(s) of leather	=	1	chicken(s)
30	square yard(s) of leather	=	1	fence (50 feet)
45	square yard(s) of leather	=	1	cow(s)
60	square yard(s) of leather	=	1	fireplace(s)
3	bushel(s) of wheat	=	2	bushel(s) of corn
5	bushel(s) of wheat	=	3	pair of shoes
2	bushel(s) of wheat	=	1	chicken(s)
10	bushel(s) of wheat	=	1	fence (50 feet)
15	bushel(s) of wheat	=	1	cow(s)
20	bushel(s) of wheat	=	1	fireplace(s)
10	bushel(s) of corn	=	9	pair of shoes
4	bushel(s) of corn	=	3	chicken(s)
20	bushel(s) of corn	=	3	fence (50 feet)

TABLE 1.1 Sample Price List for Trading Post in a Relatively Simple Barter Economy (*Continued*)

10	bushel(s) of corn	=	1	cow(s)
40	bushel(s) of corn	=	3	fireplace(s)
6	pair of shoes	=	5	chicken(s)
6	pair of shoes	=	1	fence (50 feet)
9	pair of shoes	=	1	cow(s)
12	pair of shoes	=	1	fireplace(s)
5	chicken(s)	=	1	fence (50 feet)
15	chicken(s)	=	2	cow(s)
10	chicken(s)	=	1	fireplace(s)
3	fence (50 feet)	=	2	cow(s)
2	fence (50 feet)	=	1	fireplace(s)
4	cow(s)	=	3	fireplace(s)

TABLE 1.2 A Somewhat-Simpler Price List for a Trading Post in a Money Economy

eggs	1 ₳
quart(s) of milk	3 ₳
square yard(s) of leather	8 ₳
bushel(s) of wheat	24 ₳
bushel(s) of corn	36 ₳
pair of shoes	40 ₳
chicken(s)	48 ₳
fence (50 feet)	240 ₳
cow(s)	360 ₳
fireplace(s)	480 ₳

connections dramatically simpler. For the *very same reason* that commerce tends to end up coalescing into a trading post somewhere near the village center, commercial transactions naturally tend to be conducted with money rather than with barter.

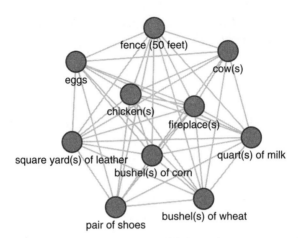

FIGURE 1.1 **"Connection web" showing all bilateral connections of 10-product barter economy**

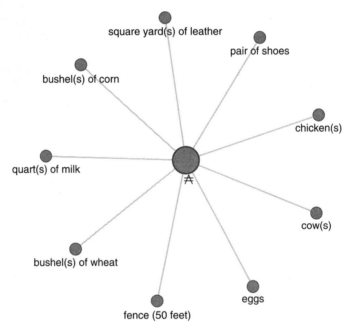

FIGURE 1.2 **Web of connections if money is an intermediate step**

TABLE 1.3   **Number of Inter-Item Connections with and without Money**

# of Products	Connections, with No Money	Connections, with Money
5	10	5
10	45	10
20	190	20
40	780	40
80	3,160	80
160	12,720	160
320	51,040	320

Money as a Store of Value

You may also have heard that one function of money is as a *store of value*. This function would be especially useful for Margo, or for anyone who wants to save, rather than consume, some of the product of his labor. We cannot long store milk, meat, or grain; our physical labors cannot be saved at all. Some goods last longer but are more difficult to resell (a fence, for example!). Certain forms of property and hard commodities such as copper or lead store much better. But once we have converted our surplus goods (beyond what is needed for the barter economy) into ingots of lead or rounds of silver, to be exchanged in the future for needed goods and services; haven't we created something that *looks* an awful lot like money?

Partly! But the physical similarities only go so far. By converting our surplus to a durable (and hopefully compact) medium, we have only created a *store of value*. This durability is one of the most crucial—and, as it turns out, one of the most fragile—aspects of money. It is this fragility, in fact, that will preoccupy us for most of this book.

In principle, this movement may go in either direction. A certain amount of lead may buy *more* shoes next year than it does now, or it may buy fewer. By converting her surplus into lead, Margo can do no worse than end up with a pile of lead, so we would say that this fact provides a limit on her risk: At the worst case, the intrinsic value of lead is still hers.

The perfect store of value for Margo would be contracts with various barter counterparties to provide future goods and services in exchange for today's milk, at today's exchange rate. Inverting the Wimpy approach of gladly paying Tuesday for a hamburger today, she would gladly pay today for the certainty of having her needs met on Tuesday.

Recall that earlier, I compared money to a battery that stores up the value of your labor, to be drawn on in the future. Obviously, we are very sensitive to how well that battery holds a charge. Money, like batteries, is often considered higher quality the better it is at holding the "charge" and drawing as much out (in terms of ability to buy things) in the future as went in, for as long as possible.

Money as a Medium of Exchange

In our third hypothetical situation, I mentioned that barter is most efficient when there is an intersection of interests between two parties who have opposite trading positions and opposite trading interests. Sometimes, a considerable amount of energy can be expended in the search for the matching interest. Another reason that trading posts or central markets, or, for that matter, securities exchanges, develop is that it lowers the search costs in looking for the opposite party. "Who will trade shoes for wheat?" Still, unless the economy is *very* simple with few goods to be exchanged, search costs rapidly escalate as the number of traded goods increases. Reflect on Margo's dilemma—she had to make four transactions to effect her ultimate goal of getting a fence. And, as noted earlier, there is the question of whether one cow will end up exchanging at the right prices to yield a fence (and only a fence) for Margo.

Using the "price list" from earlier in the chapter, we can see the potential problem:

Goal: 1 fence	
Cost of 1 fence:	$\frac{1}{2}$ fireplace
Cost of $\frac{1}{2}$ fireplace:	6 pair shoes
Cost of 6 pair shoes:	30 sq yards of leather
Cost of 30 sq yards of leather:	$\frac{2}{3}$ cow

How does one get two-thirds of a cow, or better yet one-half of a fireplace? If we demand only whole numbers, assuming that these items are only divisible down to single units, then it becomes an exercise in finding the common denominator. Here is the smallest round number of fences Margo can get, with only round numbers of items in exchange:

Sell 4 cows	Get 180 sq yards of leather
Sell 180 sq yards of leather	Get 36 pair shoes
Sell 36 pair shoes	Get 3 fireplaces
Sell 3 fireplaces	Get 6 fences

Of course, in the real world fences are divisible by length, but that turns out not to matter here. The problem is that some of the intervening steps, such as a fireplace, are *not* divisible. Some (like a cow) are technically divisible, but create other problems such as waste (if we chop up the cow, which is the only way I can think of to get two-thirds of a cow).

This gets ridiculously simple, if we introduce money. Using the price list from earlier in the chapter:

Margo sells 1 cow for 360 Ⱥ.
Margo buys 1 fence for 240 Ⱥ.
Margo has a balance of 120 Ⱥ to use for future purchases.

Ta-da! The other actors in the exchange are not left out: Tessa can sell her leather and buy her cows, Minnie can sell a fireplace and buy shoes, and so on. Notice how much simpler this transaction gets, not only for search costs but also because the money unit here makes the parts of the transaction more easily *divisible*. That is, it is much simpler to split 360 ⚚ into thirds than to split a cow!

It is important that a medium of exchange be divisible to reasonably small units, so that even small commercial transactions can occur. Today, of course, much money exchanges hands electronically, where it is almost arbitrarily divisible: You can easily buy mutual fund shares, for example, that are priced down to fractions of a cent. For convenience, banks round to the nearest penny, but the only reason they do so is because the degree of divisibility isn't universally smaller than one penny, so that you can wire money out of your account to the tune of $314.15; but if you tried to wire $314.15927, then the wire transaction would likely end up cheating someone out of the fractional penny.

When one combines the characteristics of an easily divisible medium of exchange with a store of value, we often end up with a societal choice to represent money with small tokens of some kind, usually made of some substance that has immutable intrinsic use value (for example, silver coins, barley, rice, or salt, all of which have been used as money at times in history). In prisons, where currency is not available, items such as cigarettes and postage stamps are sometimes used as money. They are easily divisible, easy to transport, easy to use as a medium of exchange, and at least a nominal store of value. Voilà: money.

Question: Why was a New York subway token better than a New York subway fare card, before tokens were phased out? Answer: A subway fare card is not easily divisible, and has no intrinsic value obvious on its face (that is, you cannot tell how many rides are left by looking at it, since a New York fare card stores that information invisibly on the magnetic strip). On the other hand, while a subway token was not easily divisible, the basic unit value was clear and the token had plain intrinsic value. In New York, before tokens were phased out in 2003, you could easily buy a newspaper at a bodega by plopping a subway token on the counter (and I occasionally did). A token was money: a fare card is not.

The Difference between Wealth, Currency, and Money

In the foregoing, I have presented a discussion of what money is and why we need it. I have pointed out that useful money can be anything that serves as a store of value, a unit of account, and a medium of exchange. Hopefully, this discussion has made clear why money is so very *useful* (a fact about which the reader was probably never in doubt) and why money tends to spontaneously develop whether or not anyone in officialdom takes any action to create it. Nobody *declared* postage stamps to be legal tender in prisons; it just happens because efficient commerce demands it. We have, then, been focusing on what is *right* with money. Before I take the other side of the argument, however, and tell you what's *wrong* with money, I want to first mention (and distinguish from money) two other concepts: *wealth* and *currency*.

Wealth is best understood as *potential*: the potential to do or to buy things that you may or may not choose to do or to buy. The difference between great wealth and relative poverty is *constraint*. Bill Gates can do or buy pretty much anything. If he wishes to build a stadium and fill it with large tuna, he can do so. He can take viola lessons from Yo Yo Ma; he can play defensive back for the Seattle Seahawks. These are things that you and I cannot do. The fact that Bill Gates *chooses* not to do these things makes him no less wealthy. He is unconstrained, in large part. The old playboy saying (or the saying, by old playboys) that "he who dies with the most toys wins" is referring to wealth, not money. Wealth need not be expressed in "toys," but the potential to buy the toys you want is what wealth is. And what we strive for is not money or currency, but wealth. As Bernadette Peters says to Steve Martin in *The Jerk*: "I don't mind losing all the money. It's losing all the stuff." She is talking about wealth.

Currency is a physical manifestation of money, in normal circumstances. It is a socially or politically defined unit of measurement of money. A dollar is currency. Are cigarettes currency? The answer is revealing about the difference between currency and money. If other people in the social unit—prison, for example—accept cigarettes as being worth a certain predefined amount of other goods and services, it is currency. For a unit of currency to be money in exchange, it must be accepted as such. The U.S. government may *say* that a dollar is legal tender for all debts, public and private; but if no one else agrees on that point, then my ATM machine is just spitting out green paper.

It is interesting to consider intersections of these concepts. For example, it is possible to have a lot of wealth without having a lot of money. Warren Buffett could empty his accounts and give all his money to charity, but as long as he owns 37 percent of Berkshire Hathaway, he has a lot of wealth. A rancher who owns 20,000 acres in West Texas may live hand-to-mouth on the basis of his monthly income and expenses, but as long as he owns that land, he is wealthy.

Less obviously, one may have a lot of money without having a lot of wealth. Consider, as an example, a software tycoon who has sold his business for $10 million, but who owes the bank $12 million. According to his bank statement, he has a lot of money. But he is quite constrained and is not wealthy. Bernie Madoff, as it turned out, had loads of money but now is extremely constrained—especially if they are making him wear leg irons in prison. In general, debt is a constraint on piles of money!

Finally, a person can have a lot of currency without having a lot of money. This seems confusing at first, since a wheelbarrow full of hundred-dollar bills is surely a lot of money as well as a lot of currency? In normal circumstances, yes, but in Weimar Germany, during their great inflation from 1922 to 1923, the wheelbarrow was worth more than the pile of currency it contained. Without the trust in the currency unit, the belief that one unit of currency today is worth one unit of *money* in exchange for something else and still will be tomorrow, the currency rapidly becomes worthless.

And, potentially, that is what's wrong with money.

Notes

1. BEA monthly personal income release, downloaded from http://www.bea.gov/newsreleases/national/pi/pinewsrelease.htm on 5/31/2015.
2. The *contract grade* is the quality of a good that must be provided in an exchange for the existing prices to be valid. It is a term most commonly associated with deliveries of physical commodities (or even securities) to satisfy a futures contract, but here I use it more broadly.
3. Since she gets more value than anyone else from the cow, she is actually engaging in a type of arbitrage or, since we're talking about cows, perhaps we should call it *herbitrage*.

CHAPTER 2

"Fiat" Money

In the first chapter, I addressed what is *right* with money. Money is crucial to the smooth functioning of any but the most simple and primitive economic systems. It greatly improves the efficiency of completing transactions and therefore greases the wheels of commerce immensely. A system of money is so important, in fact, that it seems to arise spontaneously. No one "invents" money. Or perhaps it could be said that *everyone* invents money. It is effectively what we call an "emergent property" of economic systems: Whether designed into it or not, money arises anywhere there is commerce. It is difficult, as a result, to find true barter systems anywhere; where it does occur, it is usually helped along by repressive tax regimes that create incentives for nonmonetary (and unrecorded, hence untaxed) exchanges. But even in such cases, barter is rare. After all, once a transaction goes "underground" and becomes part of a truly black market economy, the need to make the transaction efficient increases. As long as the transaction is not recorded for tax purposes, enterprising black marketers still resort to money. No checks, please—cash only!

But not all money is created the same. A subway token can be used as money, but is not a very practical unit of account. Cigarettes can be used as money, but if they get wet they will be a poor store of value (most money, as it happens, will suffer from too much liquidity, but not in this sense!). And large rocks can serve (and have served) as money, but they are an inconvenient medium of exchange.

Some money, in short, is better than other money.

What are some desirable characteristics, as opposed to the three main *functions*, of money? I have mentioned a few so far: divisibility, for one; durability, for another; portability, for a third. I have not yet mentioned *credibility*, which is perhaps the most important characteristic of all.

The word *credibility* literally means "the quality of inspiring belief in." Specifically, what is required of a monetary system, in any transaction, is that both sides believe the medium of exchange has a particular value, and that that value is *universal* (it isn't worth more when used by Margo than when used by Olaf) and reasonably *immutable* (the value doesn't change much from one transaction to the next). Margo and Olaf will only use ₳ as a medium of exchange if they are both fairly sure that Tessa will also. For if Margo gives money to Olaf for her fence, Olaf needs to be confident that he is getting the correct value in exchange—which depends critically on whether other vendors will accept ₳. Suppose they won't? Then what does Olaf have but a pile of ₳ coins or bills?

Where does credibility come from? How does money gain credibility? Two ways: by *being* and by *doing*.

The most direct way for money to be credible is to have some intrinsic value. We can easily imagine why postage stamps can be used as money. Everybody needs to mail letters from time to time (especially in prison), so we naturally (and reasonably) believe that the next guy will accept stamps as a medium of exchange. And we reasonably believe that people *tomorrow* will still need stamps, and so stamps can be a reasonable store of value. Stamps are credible simply by being.

By contrast, think of that friend of yours. When Larry asks to borrow your lawnmower and says he will return it tomorrow, how do you decide whether he is likely to do what he says?

If Larry has a history of always doing what he says, then you will find his promise credible. If Larry has a history of being a flake, you probably will not. If you have just recently met Larry, you might also place a fair weight on what other people say about him. In this way, Larry has gained credibility (or lost it) by doing. Money, similarly, *may* have credibility because people recognize it has served its purpose well in the past—no one at Burger King has ever refused to sell you fries in exchange for a few round pieces of metal or decorated pieces of paper, because those tokens have been accepted in the past for as long as the people in the transaction can remember!

Which of these two sources of credibility is more durable? Clearly, *being* beats *doing*. Nothing will happen in the foreseeable future to the utility of stamps for mailing a letter from prison. But Larry could flake out at a moment's notice. And credibility is a one-way street, for the most part. An old maxim in the bond market holds that your reputation is not like a boomerang: Once you throw it away, it doesn't come back.

It can happen as well that money loses credibility temporarily because it appears in new forms (Larry's son comes over to borrow the mower, allegedly for dad). I remember some years ago, my family went to a fast-food restaurant and in paying for the meal my father presented, among other currency, a $2 bill. At the time, the $2 bill was a new denomination (first issued in the current form in 1976). The cashier took the money to count it, but when he got to the $2 note he smiled as one who has gotten a subtle joke might smile, handed the bill back, and said, "I don't think we accept those." It took some persuasion, and calling over the manager, to convince the cashier that this was not a prank but yes, actually a bill worth two dollars, which should be accepted as such! He had never seen a $2 bill, and so in his mind it had earned no credibility by doing. Similar problems were reported on the rollout of the Susan B. Anthony dollar in 1979, and of the Sacagawea dollar in 2000.

If there is no intrinsic value, it is not automatic that money will become credible. A promise by itself has no intrinsic value. I can't eat it, drink it, or use it in any way. So for money based *only* on doing, it's the chicken-and-egg principle at work: If no one accepts the monetary unit, how will it develop credibility? And if it is not credible, how will it be accepted as a monetary unit? Enter the currency issuer.

Issuing Currency

Commodity-backed currencies were the first sorts of currency. Because carrying around large quantities of gold, silver, or other commodities was too bulky, it made sense to substitute for such commodities with certificates representing their ownership. Essentially, a person presented to his economic counterparty a note attesting to his ownership of the commodities offered in exchange. However, instead of actually presenting gold or silver, the buyer transferred ownership of the commodities by giving the note to the seller.

Do you think this is ancient history? A quaint, antiquated system no one uses any longer in a world of fiat money? Think again. This is very similar to the method used to sell a car today: the seller transfers a piece of paper representing ownership of the car (known as the car's *title*) to the buyer. The car need not be present for the transaction to occur. And did you know that there is a lively market for physical industrial metals (tin, lead, copper, and so on) in which counterparties buy and sell, or simply swap, warehouse receipts that represent ownership of a certain amount of metal in a certain physical location? If you own lead in Liverpool and you need lead in Rotterdam, it is far easier to find someone with the opposite problem than it is to move tons of lead. These two examples, the car and the industrial metals, illustrate the essence of how a commodity currency works in practice: The paper changes hands, but the physical commodity stays locked in a vault somewhere.

Now, for this to work efficiently in practice for small amounts, as in a commodity-backed currency, of course the commodity must exist somewhere. Although such currencies are backed by commodities, and so have value by being rather than doing, trust is still vitally important. If I accept a note from you that claims gold is on deposit somewhere, I want to know who is vouching for the veracity of the note! So it is only natural that banking institutions were important issuers of notes such as these, which typically could be redeemed for gold or silver coins, when they were in circulation. After all, banks had the vaults!

It is true! Once upon a time, people actually trusted banks!

Now, if there is no barrier to entry, then there is no reason that any bank couldn't issue such notes. In fact, any bank *did* issue such notes and there was in the early 1800s an absolute riot of different "currencies" in circulation in the United States. You may imagine that this caused problems when different issuers, of different levels of respectability, were issuing notes of similar denominations. Given a choice between two $5 notes, one of which is a promise from a top-flight financial institution and one a promise from a bank of more shady character, any party to a transaction is going to prefer the former. In the same way that someone today will prefer to own bonds in a AAA-rated institution rather than bonds from an institution which is only rated B—causing the AAA-rated bond to trade at a higher price—these two $5 notes will be exchangeable for different quantities of goods. This violates the requirements I mentioned earlier for money whose value is *universal* and *immutable*.

Government as Issuer

Governments have an incentive to establish clean, well-functioning economic systems, so it is only natural that national governments would want to control and standardize issuance of currency, ostensibly to improve economic efficiency. The first central bank to issue notes backed by a promise to pay in gold on demand was the Bank of England in 1695. In the United States, several attempts to regulate and replace privately issued bank notes failed before finally, in 1862, it became possible to do business using U.S. notes as currency. (By that time, the English Parliament had already restricted private institutions from issuing new banknotes, leaving *only* the Bank of England as an issuer of currency.)

Although there are advantages to being a government entity chartered with the official task of producing notes to act as legal tender currency, private issuers of currency still exist—although they are exceedingly rare.

Fiat

Obviously, for convenience, a paper bill that can be exchanged for a commodity has a big advantage over actually carrying around bars of gold or silver, bales of leather, or crates of cigarettes. But the disadvantage, from the standpoint of the issuer, is that they somewhat limit the ability of issuers to live beyond their means.

A government, when it issues a coin or a commodity-backed bill, receives in exchange an amount of raw commodity approximately equal to the denomination of the note. Alternatively, it can issue the bill in payment of its debts without holding any of the commodity into which it can be redeemed, but this is self-limiting. If holders of the currency begin to question whether a sufficient amount of the commodity is available to meet redemptions, they may begin to present the currency for redemption in exchange for the commodity that backs it.

There are three possible endgames to such a run.

The first possible outcome is that the redemption of currency stops early, and no damage is done to the general confidence that the currency's backing is sound.

The second possible outcome is that the run stops after a significant amount of redemption occurs, but all redemptions are in fact fulfilled with the commodity. In that case, trust in the money unit may remain, but the removal of a significant amount of the money of circulation can lead to substantial economic contraction. Some of the panics of the late 1800s in the United States were caused in part not by fears of convertibility but by unintended consequences attendant on the exchange of notes for gold, which caused sudden contraction of the circulating currency. This is not a good outcome, but the system can recover.

The third possible outcome is that the redemptions are not fully met. In this case, commerce can collapse as trust in the medium of exchange evaporates and the economic system is reduced in a stroke to simple, primitive barter.

Because of the threat of such outcomes, governments which issue currency backed by something physical face an inherent limitation on monetary expansion. It is a soft limitation, but a limitation nonetheless. They care about the amount of physical notes in circulation relative to the amount of commodity held (for example, in the form of gold bars in Fort Knox). The higher the amount of notes relative to the amount of commodity held, the greater is the risk of calamity. Accordingly, the supply of money in circulation is, to some degree, limited. I will make the importance of this point clear later, but for now just recognize that a promise has more weight if the promise can demand performance. "Trust, but verify" is an old Russian proverb most closely associated in the West with Ronald Reagan; this maxim also holds in the world of money.

Now consider the case of true fiat money, which is money backed only by a promise. The question is: a promise of what? If you take your ten-dollar bill to the Treasury and demand that it be redeemed, what will you get? Most likely, you will be met with a polite smile and two $5 bills. The promise of the currency issuer is a promise that it will accept the money, for it is "legal tender for all debts, public and private," as it says on U.S. currency itself. But the government cannot coerce the validity of the money in *private* exchange. It can't guarantee that when Margo transacts with Olaf, Olaf will accept the bills. And so confidence in the currency is not the first line of defense, followed by intrinsic value; it is the only line of defense.

Let's consider the possible crisis-escalation stages in such a case. Because there is no redemption of the currency for anything intrinsically valuable, there is no run for redemption. The first and second outcomes I discussed, which apply to commodity-backed money, cannot happen. This is actually *bad* news because there is no early-warning system that confidence in the monetary unit itself is compromised. The outcomes are binary: Either people believe that the money is accepted by other people, or they do not. Either everyone believes in the medium of exchange, or they do not. Failures are unlikely to be partial, with money accepted by some people and not accepted by others. Failures are likely to be total. It is the Emperor's New Clothes phenomenon: As long as everyone mutually agrees to honor the illusion, all is well. But once one person points and laughs, the illusion is totally broken and cannot be restored.

It is important to understand, I think, that the timing of this sort of structural failure may be generally predictable but is not specifically predictable. That is, in the same way that when you bend a wooden board, you know that it will break but cannot say when it will break; the timing of the breakdown of fiat systems is impossible to predict precisely.

The effect on policymakers of this no-early-warning setup is to create a tendency to sloppiness. While central bankers and government officials understand the importance of a sound and respected currency, small failures are not often "punished" by markets (at least, not immediately). Accordingly, the tendency is to allow small failures to creep into the conduct of monetary and fiscal policy operations. I will discuss later how this tendency toward laziness manifests, and what it leads to.

CHAPTER 3

The Role of Central Banks and the (Limited) Power of Monetary Policy

Central banks were established to be caretakers of the currency and of the economic system generally. The Bank of England in the late 1600s was established primarily to be the issuer of currency. The original legislative mandate of the Federal Reserve, in 1913, was to "furnish an elastic currency" and to help smooth commercial transactions by "discount[ing] notes, drafts, and bills of exchange arising out of actual commercial transactions" (as opposed to speculative finance). Over the years, the power and responsibility of central bankers expanded, and they became more and more activist. Partly this happened because elected bodies found it expedient to delegate difficult chores to an entity whose members do not stand for election. That these elements of its mandate are fundamentally in conflict is a topic I addressed at length in my book *Maestro, My Ass!*; but for our purposes here, the essential point is that central banks have become more activist over the years, as they tried to solve problems that, frankly, it isn't within their ability to solve.

Central banks have few tools at their disposal, and these tools can only accomplish certain tasks. You can't use a hammer to saw a piece of wood in half! As I mentioned earlier, in a world of commodity-backed money, the limitations on a central bank are inherently tighter. But in a fiat world, these limitations are loosened and policymakers can become sloppy, take shortcuts, and try to use their tools in ways for which they were never intended.

What Monetary Policy Can and Cannot Do

The fundamental theorem of monetarism is represented by a deceptively simple formula:

$$MV \equiv PQ$$

The triple-equals sign means that this is an identity, true by definition. What this formula means, in words, is merely that the amount of money spent on goods and services equals the amount of goods and services sold. Obviously, that must be true!

The left side of the equation has two parts. M represents the quantity of money in circulation. Though there are many ways to count money—we might include only currency, for example, or we might include savings accounts, checking accounts, money market funds, etc.—one key part of the definition that is often overlooked is the "in circulation" part. Many mistakes of analysis over the last few years, such as predictions of hyperinflation to follow hard on the heels of the "quantitative easing" by major central banks, are due to the error of overlooking the point that until money enters into the economic system, to be used in commerce, it is inert (more on this in Part II!).

The second part of the left-hand side of the equation is V, the "velocity" of money. Money velocity is simply the number of times in a year that each unit of money is spent. This makes intuitive sense: If the money supply consists of five thousand one-dollar bills, and each one is spent three times per year (Margo pays Olaf, who buys from Minnie, who purchases from Carlos), then $3 \times \$5,000 = \$15,000$ is the total amount of money spent on goods and services that year. The concept is easy but hides much complexity. Money velocity is not constant (and it is a myth that Milton Friedman said it was), and it isn't random, and to some extent it *is* predictable. But it is almost impossible to measure directly more on velocity later).

On the right-hand side of the equation are the letters P and Q. The letter P represents the price level; Q represents quantity, real output. In plain English terms, Q is something conceptually like the numerical amount of goods and services produced, and P is something like the average price paid for these items. If I buy four apples and pay $2 each for the apples, then the apple vendor has sold me $8 worth of goods and I can represent this as $4 \times \$2$.

The importance of the equation is that policymakers control (somewhat) the left side of the equation, and the desired outcomes are expressed on the right side of the equation. Changes in the price level P are called inflation, and changes in Q are called real growth. In principle, the idea is that if the central bank carefully controls M and V, it can get the P and Q it wants.

But the devil, as always, is in the details. And not many policymakers these days spend enough time worrying about the very important details!

One very, very important detail is that policymakers do not control the *mix* of P and Q that they get. The Fed, for example, can manipulate M fairly well, and can influence V. But if MV doubles, the mix of P and Q that is output is not under its control. In recent years, though, the Federal Reserve has *behaved* as if increases in money would lead automatically to higher growth. There is no reasonable basis for that belief.

A pure monetarist believes that in the long run, manipulations in M only affect P, the price level. And there is very strong

FIGURE 3.1 **The price level follows the GDP-adjusted quantity of money.**
Source: Bureau of Economic Analysis; Federal Reserve Bank of St. Louis; Milton Friedman and
Anna J. Schwartz, *Monetary Statistics of the United States* (New York: Columbia University,
1970); Robert H. Rasche, "Demand Functions for Measures of U.S. Money and Debt," in
Financial Sectors in Open Economies: Empirical Analysis and Policy Issues, edited by Peter
Hooper et al. (Washington, DC: Board of Governors of the Federal Reserve, 1990), p. 159.

evidence in support of this belief. Figure 3.1 shows the price
level in the United States, plotted against the amount of money
(specifically, the M2 measure) divided by GDP over time.

The amount of money is adjusted by the level of GDP
because we can algebraically change $MV \equiv PQ$ into $P \equiv MV/Q$.
Thus, M/Q is also plotted on the figure, with 1980 = 10 in both
cases to standardize them. This means that deviations between
the two lines represent fluctuations in money velocity over
time—because it's an identity, if we plotted P versus MV/Q,
rather than versus M/Q, the lines would perfectly overlap and
there would be no reason to show the chart. Plotting it this

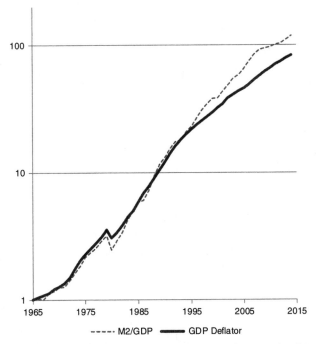

FIGURE 3.2 **Money and prices are also tightly related in South Africa. And everywhere else.**
Source: Federal Reserve Economic Data, St. Louis Fed

way, we can establish the validity of my assertion that there is very strong evidence in support of the belief that the quantity of money—relative to the size of the economy, of course—is directly related to the price level.

You can see that for a hundred years, if you knew in advance the quantity of money and the total output of the nation on any given day, you could make a pretty decent prediction of the price level. Moreover, this relationship holds for any currency for which we have good data. As an example, Figure 3.2 covers a somewhat shorter time period for South Africa (but notice there has been vastly more inflation in South Africa since 1965 than in the United States since 1913).

Now, if in the long run changes in the money supply are essentially fully reflected in the price level P, what is happening to the other part of the right side of the equation? What determines Q? Are we saying that when the Bank of Japan or the Federal Reserve or any other central bank pumps up the money supply it has no effect on growth?

Yes. That is precisely the view of a pure monetarist.

Think of what it would mean if increases in the money supply affected real growth. That would imply that if we doubled the number of dollars in everyone's bank account, people would spend more and the economy would boom. But, if we were to do that and double the amount of money that *everyone* has, then no one is really any better off, are they? Everyone has the exact same share of the wealth of the society that they had before we made the adjustment. It isn't rational that they would then expect to exchange their same-sized share for a larger share of the output of the society.

This effect is called *money illusion*. The theory says that if economic actors are fully rational, they will recognize that the increase in money lowers the value of each transactional unit of money (dollar); and so the increase in M will be fully mirrored in P. If economic actors are at least somewhat stupid or naïve, and take the increase in the money in their bank account as an actual increase in wealth, they'll spend more and the real economy will benefit.

It is, at root, an empirical question. How do people actually respond to changes in their monetary wealth that merely reflect increases in the general quantity of money in the economy?

The evidence of the last few years, and in general, is that this effect is pretty weak. It is harder than you might think to fool people by giving them more monetary units while lowering the value of each one. Consumers are attuned to prices, and it is hard to get them to notice an increase in their wealth while at the same time ignoring an increase in the cost of living. I suspect that's because most people judge the balance in their checking account in two ways. First, they notice when the balance itself is increasing over time, which is what is required for money illusion to have a chance of working. But second, and significantly, they notice that each month the checks they write take more out of the balance than they previously did. That is, their reference point is not just the balance itself, but the interplay of balances and consumption. This makes it hard to fool them with money illusion.[1]

If there *is* money illusion, then increases in MV will be reflected in P *and* Q, and the more money illusion there is then the more of Q and the less of P you will get: a good deal. But if there is no money illusion, or very little, then when MV increases you get more P and less Q: a bad deal. Later, I will talk about the way that most central banks generally view this question, but based on the evidence we have seen so far, it appears that money illusion is weak and temporary. And if that is true, it is a big error for a central bank to behave as if its actions on the left side of the monetarist equation can affect growth.

The level of real growth in the long run is affected by demographics[2] and the level of government regulation, and in the shorter run by fiscal policy although this mostly just moves demand and growth to one period (when fiscal deficits are expanding) from another (when fiscal deficits are contracting).

Let's also say a few words about monetary velocity, which is an often ignored variable when it comes to central bank policy. A central bank such as the Federal Reserve ordinarily controls fairly directly the quantity of money in circulation, although probably not currently. (I will discuss this later in the where-are-we-now portion of the book.) It does this, in ordinary times, by buying or selling securities. When it desires that the money supply increase, it buys securities from private holders. If it buys a bond, for example, it electronically credits the account of the seller with the amount of money due in the exchange, and just like that money is created where none was before. Similarly, to decrease the money supply it sells securities, and when it settles the transaction it electronically debits the account of the security holder. Shorter-term adjustments in the money supply are made by borrowing and lending securities, rather than buying and selling. The mechanism by which this changes the amount of money in circulation is well understood, and central banks are pretty good in normal times at adjusting the circulating money supply.

But central banks do not specifically target money velocity, which is curious. While precise adjustments in velocity cannot be made, the direction can be influenced easily. (I believe that the real problem is that there is a shortage of true monetarists in central bank circles today.) We actually understand quite a bit about why velocity changes. Despite what you may have heard, (a) velocity is not constant, (b) it is not random, and (c) the main cause of movements in velocity is not changes in consumer or investor confidence—"animal spirits," as it were.

Velocity is the inverse of the demand for real cash balances. The discussion of this point is beyond our scope in this book, but readers who want a more in-depth treatment can read Milton Friedman's *Money Mischief*. What we know is this: When interest rates are high, and stock prices are low, individuals and businesses work hard to avoid holding cash. They lend it by buying bonds to firms that will spend it; or they invest it, by buying equities, giving money to firms that are expanding; or they simply spend it. But the money does not sit around in cash, doing nothing, for very long. This means that the velocity of money is high when interest rates are high, and the demand for cash is concomitantly low.

On the other hand, when interest rates are low and stock prices high, the disadvantage to holding boring cash is much less and, hence, people hold more of it. Cash on corporate balance sheets and in investor accounts rises; velocity falls. This is not mere theory—Figure 3.3 shows the striking connection between interest rates on five-year government securities and money velocity.

You can see that interest rates and money velocity are closely related. This has another implication that is potentially ominous presently. If interest rates fall, then money velocity falls, which means *MV* tends to decelerate, which means that

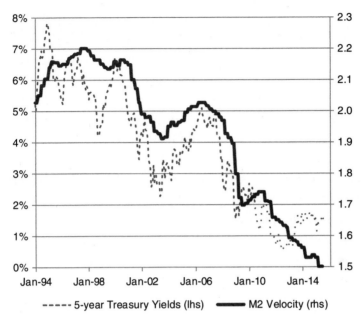

FIGURE 3.3 **Interest rates are the primary driver of changes in money velocity.**
Source: Federal Reserve; Bloomberg

nominal GDP (and, mostly, inflation) tends to decelerate. Lower inflation often prompts lower interest rates, which causes lower money velocity, and so on in a virtuous cycle. This cycle was at work in the 1990s and 2000s, as inflation, interest rates, and money velocity fell in tandem. Far from being the result of a heroic effort on the part of central banks to "anchor inflation expectations," the decline in inflation was largely a natural process. The Fed mainly gets credit for not screwing it up.

The ominous part is that we are currently near the lowest levels interest rates can reasonably attain. In fact, by the time you read this the U.S. Federal Reserve may already be raising interest rates and the long bull market in bonds may be over. The virtuous cycle then is likely to become a vicious cycle, with higher interest rates leading to higher money velocity, causing higher inflation, provoking higher interest rates, and so on. I will discuss in a later section of this book the question of where we are presently, where we are likely going, and my prescription for central banking at this juncture.

For now, know this: Monetary policy has very narrow power and should be used narrowly. Central banks can affect the supply of money, and can affect interest rates and therefore velocity either indirectly (by controlling liquidity conditions, which task is normally bound up with the management of the money supply), or directly (fixing interest rates by being prepared to lend or borrow at some declared level). With these tools, in the absence of money illusion, the *only* thing a central bank can really accomplish, as Figure 3.1 showed, is to target the price level over time.

Thus, given this limited suite of tools, the proper role of a central bank is to pursue the limited goal of near-stability of prices. By moderating the increase in the money supply, a central bank can seek equilibrium in interest rates, velocity, and inflation—all at low levels. A central bank may also police market institutions such as banks, and be the lender of last resort in this role—but this is a task that is distinct from management of the money supply and interest rates.

What a central bank cannot do is to energize real growth. Sharply increasing the money supply and cutting interest rates can change the dynamics of M and V, and hence PQ, but again, I have to point out that unless there is significant money illusion, the change in MV mainly shows up in P, after changes in Q, which are caused by other things. In a financial crisis, the best thing a central bank can do is keep money growth and interest rates as stable as possible, and stand as a lender of last resort for banks and other financial institutions so that bankruptcies and unwinds occur in a controlled rather than in a chaotic fashion. And in a simple recession, which provokes declines in asset prices but doesn't threaten financial markets or institutions, the best thing a central bank can do is keep a firm hand on the tiller and promote stability through business-as-usual.

After the stock market crash on October 19, 1987, the Federal Reserve issued a simple statement saying, "The Federal Reserve, consistent with its responsibilities as the Nation's central bank, affirmed today its readiness to serve as a source of liquidity to support the economic and financial system." That was all. Forty-one minutes after the terror attacks of 9/11, the Fed sent a message over the Fedwire saying the fund transfer system (over which virtually all money between banks is transferred) was "fully operational" and would not close at the usual time but remain open until "an orderly closing can be achieved." At noon that day, the FOMC issued a statement saying the Federal Reserve System was "open and operating" and that the discount window was "available to meet liquidity needs." Before the market reopened, the Fed held a conference call among primary dealers and made clear that shenanigans in the repo market would not be tolerated.[3]

While the Fed also provided ample liquidity in both cases, the liquidity was temporary and was more meant to compensate from any unusual glitches in the system that would slow down money transfers. The goal of the Fed in both cases was simply to help maintain calm. The behavior of the central bank in the late-2000s credit crisis, though, was much different, and I will discuss this later.

It takes great discipline for a central banker to pursue such simple goals. The Federal Reserve chairman is commonly called the second-most-powerful person in the world, after the U.S. president, and it takes enormous self-control to eschew the use of such power. It takes realizing that monetary policy should be boring, and that the use of monetary policy tools is more likely to cause harm than good in many circumstances.

With so much power in the hands of so few, and with so few checks on this power, the natural concern—which has been perpetually present since the founding of the Federal Reserve in 1913—has been about what happens if central banks are incompetent or, worse, malfeasant? This fear has led, among other things, to the rise of competing monetary systems in recent years in which the role of a central bank is reduced to an automatic process. Enter the crypto-currencies.

Notes

1. There is some experimental evidence of monetary illusion operating in contrived settings. See for example Shafir, Eldar; Diamond, Peter; and Amos Tversky, "On Money Illusion," *The Quarterly Journal of Economics*, 112 (2), May 1997, pp. 341–374. But in *actual* settings, and with long-term data, the money illusion effect seems very small. It is likely the case that in the short term it works but in the long run it doesn't, showing that you can fool all of the people some of the time but you can't fool all of the people all of the time. Monetarily speaking, that is.
2. See, for example: Robert D. Arnott and Denis B. Chaves, "Demographic Changes, Financial Markets, and the Economy," *Financial Analysts Journal* 68 (1), (Jan/Feb 2012), pp. 23–46.
3. The author was one of many, many market participants on this call.

CHAPTER 4

Bitcoin: A Solution and a Different Problem

In an interview with the Cato Institute, Milton Friedman said, "We don't need a Fed...I have, for many years, been in favor of replacing the Fed with a computer [which would, each year] print out a specified number of paper dollars" to increase the money supply in a regular way. "Same number, month after month, week after week, year after year."[1]

Although the crypto-currencies were not developed specifically in response to Friedman's suggestion, it is hard to think about sharply circumscribing the powers of a central bank without thinking about Friedman's suggestion, and hard to think about Friedman's suggestion without asking whether crypto-currencies are the solution.

Milton Friedman was a vocal opponent of the need for a central bank; he once remarked that his suggestion to replace the FOMC with a computer was only his preference because the Fed already existed; he would have preferred to have no central bank at all. "The Fed has had very few periods of relatively good performance," he continues. "For most of its history, it's been a loose cannon on the deck, and not a source of stability."[2]

What is a crypto-currency? Many readers may be more familiar with bitcoin, which is one type (and the most successful to date) of crypto-currency, but other forms of this concept have been around since the mid-1990s. The basic idea behind such crypto-currencies is to create a decentralized, mechanical issuance system to control the amount of the "currency" in circulation, as well as to provide methods for direct peer-to-peer transfer of the unit. However, this latter characteristic is certainly not unique to crypto-currencies (I can also hand you a dollar or a yen or a peso, in a "peer to peer" exchange). The main distinguishing characteristic of these systems is that the management is decentralized, automatic, and stable.

Since bitcoin is the most successful of the crypto-currencies, and since *bitcoin* is shorter and easier to write than "crypto-currency," I will henceforth refer to bitcoin's characteristics. However, since bitcoin might someday be replaced by another crypto-currency, readers should consider these comments as applicable to the class of crypto-currencies, rather than only to bitcoin.

Bitcoin solves one problem and allays one fear of strong-money advocates: the possibility that a lazy or incompetent central bank could do great damage to holders of money in a fiat system. Bitcoin was developed in 2009, and relies on complicated algorithms that encode and verify the entire history of bitcoin transactions in one long record call the *block chain*. Bitcoin can be earned by doing work on the block chain, repeatedly verifying transactions and keeping the block chain consistent; the amount of bitcoin earned for a given amount of work is controlled by an algorithm that gently increases the total amount of bitcoin outstanding. So, as with the forms of money we discussed early in this book, bitcoin is earned in exchange for work—in this case, work that would be hard to barter with since it involves processing cycles on a computer. The algorithm ensures that the total amount of bitcoin increases only gradually over time. There is no role for a central bank. The money supply does what the algorithm says it will do.

Bitcoin had a meteoric rise to what the supporters call respectability and the detractors call sensationalism. In 2009, no one had heard of bitcoin and you could buy one bitcoin for less than a nickel. Four years later, *Forbes* magazine was calling 2013 the "Year of the bitcoin"[3] and giving a Christmas present of one bitcoin would have cost you $710 (after peaking at $1,137 per bitcoin in late November 2013).

But is bitcoin money? Calling it a virtual currency, or a digital currency, or a crypto-currency doesn't make it money. At some level, it is of course money in the same sense as cigarettes are to prison inmates. It serves as a medium of exchange, a store of value, and a unit of account—but only within the special community that already accepts bitcoin as credible. You can't use bitcoin to buy groceries at Kroger, for example. Your neighbor is unlikely to accept bitcoin if your kid breaks a window. It is not yet broadly a credible currency. It doesn't have universal value because not everyone believes that everyone else will accept bitcoin.

Remember what I said earlier about how a currency gains credibility: It can gain credibility by being, or by doing. Which is it for bitcoin?

By creating perceived scarcity, relative to currencies that are managed in a more ad-hoc manner, bitcoin may create a higher price for the currency. But it doesn't create trust any more than people "trusted" high-flying internet stocks in 1999. Perhaps they trusted that the stocks would keep going up, but they didn't trust the companies simply because the stocks were going up. Does trust in bitcoin come from its being? No, because nothing is "behind" bitcoin. Bitcoin cannot be melted down, or redeemed for gold, silver, or anything else with intrinsic value. Trust in bitcoin, to whatever extent it exists, must come *from doing*. In this case, trust is a result of the algorithm.

As an aside, bitcoin's algorithm is not even especially conservative. Figure 4.1 shows the total amount of bitcoin in circulation. Figure 4.2 shows the year-over-year change in the bitcoin "money supply" versus the year-over-year change in the M2 measure of the U.S. money supply.

But whether the trust in the bitcoin unit is rational or not among the community in which it is generally accepted, the more relevant point here is that it is trust that comes from doing, not being. Bitcoin is no less "fiat" money than is the U.S. dollar, the euro, or the yen.

This is important because in early 2014 we saw a great example of what can happen when trust in fiat money is shaken.

Mt. Gox was an exchange that had evolved to transact bitcoins; in late 2013 it was handling around 70 percent of all bitcoin transactions. Note that it wasn't *issuing* bitcoins or *guaranteeing* bitcoins, just trading them. But there were hints of troubles. In June of 2013, Mt. Gox temporarily

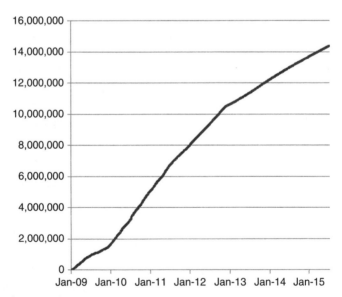

FIGURE 4.1 **Total number of bitcoins in circulation**
Source: Blockchain.info

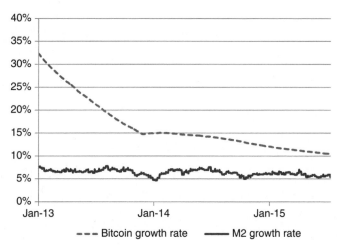

FIGURE 4.2 **Rate of change of bitcoin money supply vs U.S. M2 money supply**
Source: Blockchain.info, Federal Reserve

suspended withdrawals in U.S. dollars; even when it resumed offering withdrawals, it was very slow to complete them. Despite this, bitcoin prices soared in the second half of 2013, leading to the *Forbes* headline I mentioned earlier.

Then on February 7, 2014, Mt. Gox suddenly announced that it was preventing withdrawals of bitcoins due to a "technical" issue; within three weeks, the exchange filed for bankruptcy and revealed it had "lost" some 850,000 client bitcoins worth, at the time, around $450 million. Whoops!

The exchange rate between dollars and bitcoins fell from $727 per bitcoin on February 7 to $466 by the end of March: a decline of 36 percent, as Figure 4.3 shows. And the value continued to decline.

In other words, prior to the implosion of Mt. Gox, 100 bitcoins would have bought $72,700 worth of stuff; at the end of March it would have taken 156 bitcoins to buy the same pile of stuff. For a U.S. investor, that works out to an annualized inflation rate of nearly 400 percent! One year later, you would have

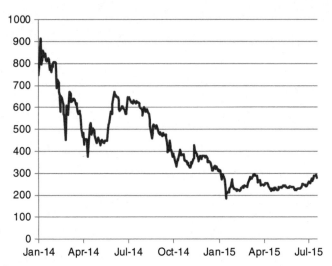

FIGURE 4.3 **Cost of one bitcoin, in US$**
Source: Bloomberg

needed 325 bitcoins to buy that pile of stuff—a one-year inflation rate of 225 percent.

This is what happens when trust is broken, for money is based entirely on trust.

Bitcoin solved one problem—the risk of lazy or incompetent central banks. But bitcoin has a very big secondary problem: It is a currency backed by nothing but trust, and it has a big credibility problem at the moment.

Maybe bitcoin can recover. Most currencies that lose credibility in this way have no chance to recover, but perhaps since bitcoin was not *widely* accepted before the Mt. Gox fiasco it might still recover as more people learn about the currency for the first time. My guess is that it will not ever become a valid and widely-accepted alternative currency, but I may be wrong.

But what I am sure of is this: I don't want to see the money *I* use every day suffer the same fate.

Notes

1. http://www.cato.org/publications/commentary/milton-rose-friedman-offer-radical-ideas-21st-century.
2. Ibid.
3. http://www.forbes.com/sites/kitconews/2013/12/10/2013-year-of-the-bitcoin/.

CHAPTER 5

How Fiat Money Dies

Money that derives value by *being*, that is money that is backed by something of intrinsic value, is not immune to problems. Its fate is tied up with the fate of the commodity that backs it. This has occasionally caused issues when the supply of commodity abruptly changes for one reason or another (better mining techniques, for example, or the introduction of money in another country backed by the same thing, so that there is suddenly less "float" of the commodity involved). But, by and large, the issues are temporary and relatively minor compared with what happens to fiat money.

It is an exaggeration to say that every fiat currency has eventually collapsed. That isn't true, because there are many such currencies extant today. However, we can say that there is a marked tendency, historically, for *dramatic* collapse in these currencies on occasion.

The most interesting case, to me, is the case of the Roman denarius, which was a silver coin used in the early Roman Empire. In 15 BC, the Roman emperor Caesar Augustus set the standard silver content for the denarius at around 95 percent. Now, it isn't so important that the denarius was 95 percent silver; any fixed percentage would do. What is important is that the silver content didn't vary tremendously. If it did, then coins with more silver (assuming that was the most valuable metal in the alloy) would be worth more than those with less silver, and the denarius wouldn't have a fixed value (and would fail the test of being a constant unit of account).

Now, obviously the denarius as I have just described it isn't a fiat currency at all. It had intrinsic value as a result of the silver content. But what is interesting is that the Roman emperors gradually debased the currency, reducing the silver content by moving to a coin that was only *plated* in silver, and the silver content was gradually reduced from there. Eventually, "the surface coating was so thin that it quickly rubbed off after the coin left the mint."[1] Most of that decline in silver content happened between the end of the reign of Commodus and the beginning of the reign of Diocletian in AD 284. During this extraordinarily violent period of empire (some 30 emperors and co-emperors ruled during that century), the concentration of silver in the denarius fell from roughly 80 percent to approximately zero.

At this point, the coin no longer had intrinsic value of note. It only had value because the emperor said so, and after 30 changes on the throne, there wasn't much trust in the emperor. Diocletian tried price controls—which were ignored—and inflation helped to fell the Roman Empire.

Other episodes with fiat money have ended similarly: gradual debasement, followed by collapse.

Debasement literally means a losing of the base: a loss of stability, value, or significance. When we talk about money, what we mean by debasement is that the monetary unit has lost value against the things that money can buy (and there is often a connotation that the change in value was intentional, as when Roman emperors decreased the concentration of silver in the coinage). If Margo was formerly able to buy a fence for 240₳, and now the same fence costs 480₳, then we would say the currency has been debased. We might also call this *inflation*, which has a less-ugly connotation regarding intentionality. Whatever we call it, historically fiat money has failed in one of three ways: slowly, suddenly, or *first* slowly and *then* suddenly.

Money fails *slowly* when lazy central banks add too much to the supply of money, causing its value in terms of "stuff" to decline. Kublai Khan, who was one heck of a conqueror but not a very good central banker, supposedly printed new currency every time he needed to pay someone. Now, that's pretty lazy, but to be fair he was reasonably good at other things. By the way, what is it with empires and fiat money?

When money fails slowly, it shows up as inflation creeping slowly higher, and eventually to levels that are uncomfortable and that impinge on ordinary decision making in the economy. Many Western economies were in that zone in the late 1970s, before their citizens pulled back from the brink and confidence in their leadership recovered. When money is failing slowly, the higher level of inflation means that money is failing in one of its three primary purposes: It is failing to be a good *store of value*. Money in this sort of environment will still function as a medium of exchange and a unit of account, but as a store of value, it suffers. No one wants to hold cash in this kind of an environment because its value is eroding too quickly.

Money fails *suddenly* when a traumatic event has a dramatic impact on the society as a whole, and consumers and investors begin to question the survival of the system itself: Germany, in the years after losing World War I, being saddled with unpayable reparations payments; the U.S. Confederacy, after Gettysburg; the nationalization of land and general corruption of the Mugabe government in Zimbabwe in the mid-2000s. In each of these cases, and in many more, inflation ran over 1,000 percent, and in some cases into the millions of percents. These numbers mean little because of their scale, but to put this in context, an inflation rate of 1,000 percent means that 90 percent of your money's value is lost every year. At an inflation rate of 12,000 percent, 90 percent of your money's value is lost every *month*. Economists call this hyperinflation, but it is essentially no more and no less than a failure of money itself.

These sorts of inflation rates don't (usually) happen because the central bank increases the money supply a hundredfold. These happen when money loses its function not only as a store of value but also as a medium of exchange. Confederate shopkeepers didn't know if the Greyback was going to be accepted by *anyone* tomorrow! In cases like this, economies turn back to barter—the financial dark ages, incredibly inefficient, but offering the comfort of knowing that a cow is still a cow, a shovel is still a shovel, and a day's work is still a day's work.

There is a third case worth considering. In Ernest Hemingway's *The Sun Also Rises*, Bill asks Mike, "How did you go bankrupt?" and Mike replies, "Two ways. Gradually and then suddenly." The death of fiat money can also happen in this way. Inept or insouciant monetary policy can lead to creeping inflation, which gradually drags at the edges of commerce until it hits a level, a *tipping point*, where economic actors begin to question whether there is a light at the end of the tunnel after all. This is a common theme in developing countries and especially common in Latin America. Consider the case of Bolivia, which in September 1976 sported a year-on-year inflation rate of 2.3 percent. Table 5.1 shows the subsequent year-end inflation rates for the next few years.

TABLE 5.1   **Annual Bolivian Inflation Rates**

1976	5.5%
1977	10.5%
1978	13.5%
1979	45.5%
1980	23.9%
1981	25.1%
1982	296.5%
1983	330.1%
1984	2,168.3%
1985	8,173.3%

Source: Instituto Nacional de Estadistica—Bolivia

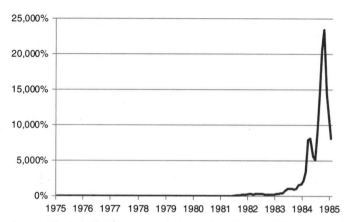

FIGURE 5.1 **Bolivian inflation 1975–1985, monthly**
Source: Instituto Nacional de Estadistica, Bolivia

I present these data in tabular format because the charts are hard to grasp. Figure 5.1 shows the Bolivian year-over-year inflation rate, monthly.

It looks like a simple case of "suddenly," in this form. But Figure 5.2 shows the same data with a logarithmic scale, so that each line as you go up the chart reflects *ten times* the rate of inflation of the previous line.

FIGURE 5.2 **Bolivian inflation 1975–1985, monthly—but in logarithmic scale**
Source: Instituto Nacional de Estadistica, Bolivia

In this format, you can see that the acceleration in inflation was relatively modest in developing country terms. Inflation was in the low double-digits in 1977 and 1978. In 1979, it accelerated to the mid-double-digits. In 1980 and 1981, inflation rates fell back to the mid-20s, but not enough progress was being made; and confidence in the monetary unit exited, stage left, in 1982.

Michael Walton, a development economist who teaches at Harvard, calculated that "27 percent of countries experiencing 40 to 60 percent inflation experience inflation over 100 percent within three years; 78 percent of countries with 100 percent inflation experience that level again within three years; and 29 percent experience inflation of over 1,000 percent in this period."[2] In short: Letting the inflationary cat out of the bag is a hell of a lot easier than getting him back in.

Another observation by Mr. Walton is worth noting here, and as we move into the next section where we discuss the current economic situation. In describing what he calls the "standard recipe" for the hyperinflation disaster, he says:

"An initial shock initiates the process: for example tax revenues fall due to an external shock, for example following a negative terms of trade shock (reduction in world prices for the country's main export commodity or increase in price of a vital import, e.g. oil or electricity). The governments usually find it impossible to cut expenditures, plus there is a natural tendency to overestimate the probability that the terms of trade shock or financing problem is temporary, e.g. governments often rely on the assumption that world prices for the export commodity will soon rise. Therefore, the government's usual reaction is to borrow from the rest of the world. If the government is wrong in its hopes and the terms of trade remain unfavorable, such a strategy will put the government in an even worse position. In addition to paying domestic expenditures, the government must now finance a growing stock of debt. Eventually foreign lending

dries up (due to a high risk of default), and indeed may go into reverse, and seignorage [ed. note: money printing to finance deficits] becomes the government's main source of financing. High inflation causes a drop in real output and a fall in the demand for real money balances, which further decreases fiscal and seignorage revenues, which sets off the race between government extracting finance through seignorage and the public responding by fleeing from money, propagating a high to hyperinflation spiral.[3]

So the recipe for this sort of transition to hyperinflation—what I call the "slowly, then suddenly" case of money failure—involves an initial shock, which leads to big deficits that are *believed* to be temporary but that turn out to be persistent, resulting in the need to finance a growing stock of debt that eventually demands monetary financing. While I do not consider hyperinflation a very likely case in the developed world, at least in the near future, I must admit that this "standard recipe" sounds chilling to me.

Where do I think we are? And where do I think we are going? In this section, I've addressed the importance of money, as well as the inherent problems and risks that are attendant with money that is backed only by the mutual trust of the citizenry. In Part 2, I will address where we have been (economically speaking) and where I believe we are likely to go.

Notes

1. Alan W. Pense, "The Decline and Fall of the Roman *Denarius*," *Materials Characterization* 29 (1992), p. 213.
2. Michael Walton, "High and Hyperinflation: Determinants and Solutions," Teaching notes for *Applications and Cases in International Development*, available at http://www.michael walton.info/wp-content/uploads/2010/11/High-and-Hyper inflation-Determinants-and-Solutions.pdf.
3. Ibid.

PART II

Where Are We Now?

In writing this section about where we have come from, economically speaking, where we are now, and where we are going, I am acutely aware that I am setting myself up like a clay pigeon for target practice. I know this because for a number of years now I have written a blog (http://mikeashton .wordpress.com) about which I routinely receive two criticisms:

1. I am too alarmist.
2. I am not alarmed enough.

I am not trying to walk any lines. I am not trying to balance between these two camps. These are my views. This also means they can change over time. So these are my views *today*, supported with charts and statistics and data. I present cases and possibilities and potential paths, but if I happen to make a point prediction it is a gut feel, a guess by another name, and probably wrong (at least in the sense that it won't be exactly right).

But that doesn't mean that you should stop reading. I think too many predictions are made, and people are too eager to be told exactly what to do. That's not my style.

When I was on Wall Street, I twice was interviewed for high-level research positions (even after I had left the research world and had become a trader). In one case, the job was as the global fixed-income research head for retail investors, and one job was as the U.S. fixed-income research head, in both cases at large institutions you have heard of. In both cases, I explained to the hiring firm that I think Wall Street research is all wrong in its approach (never mind its conclusions). Researchers write as if they are trying to give clients the "right answers"—what is going to happen, and when. If you have seen this research, you know that their track record is not particularly confidence-inspiring. Even allowing, perhaps too generously, that most researchers are not mere shills for the banks' equity or bond sales teams, it is still a bad model. The best researchers are going to be right about general direction a little more than half the time, and even then they'll hardly ever be *exactly* right. When they miss, they will sometimes miss badly. And then what good have you done for the client *or* the bank?

A much better model is to try and ask the right questions. A good analyst can do this nearly 100 percent of the time. And asking the right questions is always valuable. "Here is the big question. We think X will happen, but if you believe Y will happen then you ought to do this instead . . . " There are analysts who do this very well—James Montier and Rob Arnott are two of the people I enjoy reading even when I disagree with their conclusions, because at least they are asking the right questions. They are in the minority, and they're not even on the sell side of Wall Street. "In short," I concluded triumphantly to the hiring managers, "Wall Street research is mostly useless."

I didn't want those jobs anyway.

My point is that in the end, my forecasts herein are less important than whether the framework for thinking about the problem helps you to understand how to prepare for the various possibilities. I will present my thoughts on that topic in Part III.

CHAPTER **6**

Don't Believe Everything You Read (But Believe Some of It)

When we talk about the failure of money, the main metric we care about in terms of things you hear about every day is *inflation*.

Before I get too far into a discussion about where inflation is, and where it is likely to head from here, I want to take a brief detour to hopefully short-circuit some of the unhelpful, distracting arguments that often arise when we talk about inflation and how it is measured.

In the United States, and in most other developed countries, the single most important measure of consumer inflation is the Consumer Price Index (CPI), which in the United States is calculated by the Bureau of Labor Statistics (BLS). It is also one of the most maligned numbers in existence, even though CPI is also one of the more carefully designed and researched numbers in the entire list of government releases. This is partly because so much is riding on it, between securities linked to non-seasonally-adjusted CPI (such as TIPS) and contracts such as Social Security and others. To some people, this just opens the door for more government shenanigans, since arguably the government stands to gain the most from monkeying with CPI. And I understand that suspicion.

But if people with lots of money on CPI didn't fundamentally believe in the veracity of the number, then the trillion-dollar-plus TIPS market would be in real trouble. Indeed, in some countries where there is better reason to doubt the government's accountability on such matters, there are private as well as public inflation indices and securities are linked to each index. (Brazil is one example.)

That doesn't mean that these investors are right, of course, but you can believe that they've looked pretty hard at the number. Sure, investors have also looked very hard at equities in 2015 and concluded that they are entitled to a very lofty multiple, so we can't just rely on what investors think. I will tell you, though, why inflation cannot possibly be as high as some folks believe it is, and why you very likely feel that inflation is higher than is being reported by the government.

What follows is an enumeration of some of the cognitive errors that people make with respect to CPI. The list isn't complete, but I think I've hit on the biggest of them.

As a first point: CPI does what it is supposed to do very well, but that might not be what you want it to do. It is not supposed to measure the average change of prices in the economy. It is closer to a cost-of-living index, which means that it is meant to answer the question "What is the cost of achieving today the standard of living actually achieved in the base period?" This is a difficult goal, since your "standard of living" must necessarily incorporate your preferences about how different goods and services are better or worse than others, and we can't directly test your preferences. All that the BLS can do is to survey prices and quantities consumed, to draw inferences about consumption patterns, and to calculate the change in prices of the consumption basket that keeps the average consumer's standard of living approximately unchanged. That's difficult, and they do it remarkably well at that.

This important point gives rise to the concept of *hedonic adjustments*, which adjust the price recorded by the BLS for a particular good to account for changes in the quality of those goods. This is a crucial adjustment for certain goods that change significantly in quality over time, such as cars, computers, and medical care (and, in the negative direction, houses as they age). But this is one source of complaints from people who don't bother to understand the CPI: People don't mentally record hedonic adjustments; people measure cash out of their pockets. So when you buy a new computer and it is lots better than the last one but costs the same, you experienced deflation in the sense that the cost of your old lifestyle—*which you no longer have*—costs less. Since you spent the same amount, it doesn't feel like deflation to you, but since your standard of living improved while the costs were unchanged, that's deflation in a cost-of-living index sense.

As a second observation: Your consumption basket may vary. For most people, the broad CPI index is a reasonable measure, but each person's consumption is different. Some people spend more on apparel and less on recreation; others are the opposite. CPI is supposed to measure the average experience, and no one is exactly average.

Finally, as a third point I will develop more fully next: There are a number of common cognitive and comprehension errors that most people make when they think about inflation. The work on the psychology of decision making by Tversky and Kahneman—the latter of whom won a Nobel Prize in Economics for his work[1]—can help us understand why. These are complex issues to evaluate, but not too hard to *understand*. Note that this is a problem somewhat peculiar to inflation statistics. With employment statistics (e.g., the unemployment rate), we have a fairly good natural sense about what "feels right" because there's an easy way to make an educated guess: For example, if we have a lot of friends who are unemployed, and more seem to be losing their jobs, then we can fairly assume the unemployment rate is high and rising. But this is very difficult to do with inflation because of the sheer computational complexity of tracking thousands of prices of things you buy, over long periods of time, in your head.

But some complaints about CPI go way beyond these innocent and entirely normal perceptual biases.

Some complaints of CPI are just silly. One website in particular has made quite a great business catering bad data to conspiracy theorists. It has a chart of what inflation would be if the BLS used 1980 methods, with the implication being that the evil government is trying to hide the 9 percent rate of inflation (the site says inflation is understated by about 7 percent). The choice of 1980 is very adept, since it was in 1982 that the BLS changed the method of computing the cost of housing to remove home investment considerations (such as the mortgage rate) and focus on the consumption value of the home (which is best represented by what it would cost to rent). This was done after much research, many public papers, and debate, and is absolutely the right way to measure inflation in the cost of housing *consumption* as distinct from changes in the value of the home as an asset. There are lots of other improvements that have been made to CPI, and they really are improvements.

We can rely on a very simple argument to *prove* that true inflation cannot be at 9 percent (but the argument involves math). I presume that most readers can recall what they were paid as a wage or salary 10 years ago, or at least can very easily figure out what their income was back then. Government statistics say that the average increase in *wages and salaries* (in the Employment Cost Index) has been about 24 percent over the 10 years from 2005Q1 to 2015Q1.

I assume that we don't think the government is exaggerating that number on the low side for some sinister reason. Now, if inflation is really running at the 9 percent or so that this particular website says it has for the last decade, then while your wages have grown 24 percent, the cost of living has risen 136 percent (the government says inflation has been more like 22 percent).

More concretely: Suppose you made $60,000 in 2005, took home $40,000 after tax, and were just breaking even with your cost of living also at $40,000. According to the government, today you ought to be making about $74,600, and if taxes were the same, your take home pay of $49,700 would leave you about $900 better off, with your cost of living about $48,800. Viscerally, this would feel like you are marginally "better off" than you were in 2005, but overall pretty close to unchanged. If, however, inflation was really at 9 percent, then your cost of living is now $94,400—around twice the value calculated using government data—and you most likely declared bankruptcy several years ago. You don't have to be able to track your receipts to see that 9 percent is not the right rate of inflation—you just need to look at the compounded outcome.

Consider a longer period of time for a more poignant comparison. The person making $30,000 and taking home $20,000 in 1985 is now making $73,300, and the current $48,900 take-home pay (two-thirds, assuming improbably that taxes were unchanged) has improved his/her standard of living somewhat as the old standard of living now costs $44,400 using CPI. Using a 7 percent higher rate of inflation, the same standard of living this person enjoyed in 1980 for $20,000 now costs $320,900; if that is correct, then the *average* person would be living in a cardboard box, in utter squalor.

That is nonsense. And by the way, it also means that housing over the decade ending in 2007 not only wasn't in a bubble; it didn't even come *close* to keeping up with inflation, and *neither did any other asset in the world.* That's worse than nonsense; it is an offensive ignorance of mathematics.

CPI is not a perfect number, and moreover, it may not be a perfect number for what you want it to do. But it does what it is supposed to do, and it does it very well.

It is a separate question, though, what inflation *feels* like. Moreover, it is very relevant. Modern monetary policy considers inflation expectations a metric of signal importance in the formulation of monetary policy. While the Taylor Rule provides a well-known heuristic for monetary policymakers that relies on actual, not expected inflation, policy discussions rely very heavily on the question of whether inflation expectations are, and will continue to be, "contained." Former Federal Reserve Chairman Ben Bernanke himself described the importance and significance of inflation expectations in a speech in 2007 by saying "Undoubtedly, the state of inflation expectations greatly influences actual inflation and thus the central bank's ability to achieve price stability."

So how does the Fed measure inflation expectations? Generally, they do so with surveys—including the Livingston survey, the Survey of Professional Forecasters (SPF), and the Michigan Survey of Consumer Attitudes and Behavior. Some of these measure the expectations of economists about CPI, which isn't really helpful—the Fed already has its staff economist forecasts, so checking a survey consisting essentially of the same people they hang out with at the club would give a false sense of security.

The Michigan survey asks consumers for their views about "the expected change in prices." But here's the problem: Normal humans are not capable of conducting in their heads the *monumental tasks* of cataloging all of the year's purchases and calculating the differences from the same basket from the year before. Price changes are not homogeneous, and this leads to seat-of-the-pants adjustments. Consider this very thorough explanation I got several years ago from a friend in response to a question I had asked about her perception of what had happened generally over the prior year to prices *she* paid:

My personal experience has been that big ticket items have gone down, but small ticket items have gone up (example fast-food ice-tea prices or Frontline for my dog). It is crazy that I spend almost $2 for a glass of ice tea that is just water and a tea bag with some ice. But the cost has gone up around 20 cents at most places in the past two years. Conversely, grocery store prices are very mixed with some real bargains, but I do see vast differences between the same good at Wal-Mart and at Kroger. Sometimes Kroger prices are 25% higher for the identical item. I stopped drinking Coke over six years ago. A bargain then was three cases for $10. I saw a display at Wal-Mart the other day of one case for $5.25. It may have had 18 cans instead of the 12 of old. It looked bigger; if so, that would indicate not much price pressure. I recently bought a fan to replace one that died. The new one was by the same company and almost identical, but cost the same after 3–4 years. Of course, I bought the first one at a department store and the second one at Wal-Mart. (FYI Wal-Mart is about the only store less than an hour and fifteen minutes from my house other than dollar stores or local hardware stores. Did you know that each Wal-Mart sets its own pricing? There can be noticeable price differences sometimes on the same item at my two nearest Wal-Marts. The slightly closer one has less competition and they told me that lets them price some goods higher than the other store.) But, TVs and computers are a lot cheaper, so much so that it has induced me to buy. My telephone and cable bills haven't changed in years. These conflicting observations made it very hard for me to answer your question.

I couldn't have said it better myself! This person had a real grasp of what she had been paying over the last couple of years for a number of products, but even so: Note that no product she mentioned represented more than a tiny fraction of her total consumption for the year. But if you really sit down and think about it, you can come to the same (non)conclusion. It is really hard to develop an analytical sense of what is happening to prices. Therefore, we tend to rely on our visceral sense of what is happening to inflation, and this is why the conspiracy website can sell its crazy talk about 9 percent inflation.

Clearly, the FOMC would like to sample the perceptions of the people who are involved in price-setting and wage-setting behavior. But consumer surveys are not ideal instruments for at least two reasons. First, as some researchers have pointed out, taking the "average" expectation obscures a lot of information and it isn't exactly clear what role the variation in expectations should play. Second, and more importantly, surveys of inflation don't work well because consumers do not discern inflation properly. Perceptions of inflation are muddied by a myriad of practical problems (such as those described so clearly by my correspondent above!) and behavioral biases that tend to impair accurate assessment of price changes. For example:

- Quality change and substitution adjustments are not recognized viscerally by consumers, although they are a necessary part of a cost-of-living index. It might also be the case that people notice downward quality adjustments ("my insurance coverage is shrinking") more than upward quality adjustments.
- Consumers have an asymmetric perception of inflation as a whole, as well, so that they tend to notice goods that are inflating faster than the overall market basket, but to notice less the goods that are not inflating as fast. This sense is enhanced by classic attribution bias: higher prices are "inflation," lower prices are "good shopping."

- Items whose prices are volatile tend to draw more attention, and give more opportunities for these asymmetries to compound, so they tend to factor more heavily into our sensation of inflation.
- People notice price changes of small, frequently-purchased items more than they notice large, infrequently-purchased items even though the latter are a bigger part of consumption basket. Gasoline is hugely important even though it's not a huge part of the basket because (a) it is purchased frequently and (b) it is volatile.
- Consumers do not viscerally record imputed costs, such as owners'-equivalent rent for homeowners, as distinct from what they see as their costs (in the case of a home, principal plus interest, taxes, and insurance). Even though the former is better for CPI, the latter (which is the pre-1983 method, basically) affects perception more directly.
- People perceive increases in income taxes as inflation, even though income taxes have nothing to do with the prices you pay in a store.

In 2012, I wrote a paper that attempted to correct for a few of these biases.[2] If we can model inflation perceptions in the way I described there then we might not only be able to identify changes in inflation perceptions but to also understand the drivers of those changes in any particular episode. The monetary policy prescription might vary if, for example, elevated perceptions of inflation were driven by an increase in taxes rather than because of an increase in the volatility of price changes in the consumption basket.

Let me return to the reason for this exercise, this time with a simple analogy. There is clearly a reason that we need to measure the CPI with as much exacting, mechanical precision as we can muster. Knowing how prices are actually changing in the economy is important for consumers, wage-earners, and investors. Similarly, it is very important to have a good thermometer that can tell you just how cold it actually is outside in Chicago in January. But before venturing outside in Chicago in January, you ought also to consider the "wind chill" or "real feel" temperature, because it has great relevance for your real-life behaviors. The "true" temperature is given by the thermometer, but in many situations the wind chill is what actually matters (it is connected more directly, in this case, to your survival chances if you underdress).

What investors and consumers are railing against, when they declare angrily that the government is "cooking up" fake inflation statistics, is that inflation doesn't *feel* as low as CPI says that it is. But in fact, inflation is. This doesn't mean that it is unimportant that inflation feels higher than it actually is. Policymakers need to know not only what prices are actually doing, but what the "real feel" inflation rate is, because it is relevant for many consumer decisions.

But, with that being said, we ought to also realize over the next chapters that the Consumer Price Index is probably the best measure we have of estimating the prices that people actually experience. You should never believe everything you read, but you need to believe this.

Notes

1. Amos Tversky likely would have shared the Nobel with Daniel Kahneman and Vernon L. Smith, but he passed away in 1996 and the Nobel is never awarded posthumously.
2. Michael J. Ashton, "Real-Feel" Inflation: Quantitative Estimation of Inflation Perceptions, *Business Economics*, 47 (1), 2012, pp. 14–26.

CHAPTER 7

Central Bankers Are Monetarists No Longer

I am somewhat sympathetic to the situation in which central bankers have been placed. Keep in mind that the soft science of economics is only a bit more than two hundred years old (contrast this with astronomy or physics, which are thousands of years old); the discipline has only become mathematical and precise in the last generation or two. So it would be unfair to economics to expect very much from it: as a mature science, economics is probably something like medicine was in the late 1800s.

Of course, it is only in retrospect that we can see that disease isn't caused by foul humors, and that many diseases are not in fact helped by leeching the patient. At the time, we are always on the cutting edge and view ourselves as very advanced. The consensus view is always, by definition, regarded as the "best" answer. In this, science is like an adolescent child who always feels so smart relative to the person he or she was a few years earlier; it is only later that we learn that we weren't as smart as we thought, and our parents really were right about a lot of things. Our younger selves always embarrass our current selves, but we rarely consider that the actions of our current self will be embarrassing to our future selves.

This is where economics is now. Economics is an adolescent science, and it makes bad decisions sometimes. The increased precision of economics, granted by the ever-increasing quantity of mathematics used by practitioners, does not imply greatly increased understanding. And yet, we have handed economists the car keys to the economy. That economists feel up to the challenge of taking a few risks, as adolescents frequently do, is not surprising. That we are willing to trust them with the keys, given the number of dents they have put in our economic automobile, is.

And so, as I say, I am somewhat sympathetic. I, too, wanted the car keys when I first got my license.

What we would like to believe about science is that it always moves forward. In the hard sciences, this is a reasonable description of reality. The nature of the experimental method and of physical proof tends to make scientific understanding of, say, physical materials move forward inexorably with few instances of backsliding (where the "new" answer is less correct than the "old" answer). For example, the heliocentric model of the universe was not "correct," but it was closer than the earth-centric model.

The social sciences, on the other hand, behave more like adolescents. They mature, but not without some mistakes along the way. In the case of economics, and of central banking as an application of macroeconomic understanding, this is exactly what has happened.

Two Big Revolutions in Central Banking

In the last 30 years there have been two huge changes in the way central bankers ply their trade. The first huge change is the movement toward greater openness and transparency. I refer to this as the *glasnost* trend, since the tendency toward central bank transparency began at about the same time as Mikhail Gorbachev began to press the Soviet Union to open up.

While it would seem that transparency is naturally a good thing, something that is always a positive to strive for, recognize that we don't behave that way in many areas of our own lives. We don't view transparency of our medical records, for example, as a good thing. And, at the risk of polluting my earlier metaphor about adolescents, we parents certainly think that some discussions about child-rearing ought not to be held in front of the children themselves. Why not? Because the children will react differently if they know the plan for them, reducing our ability to nudge them surreptitiously into the proper behavioral outcome. [To my children, if you are reading this: not you, of course!]

In a similar way, I believe, transparency in a central bank is a negative for financial markets. Note that I am not talking about operational transparency. Oversight of central bank activity by the legislature is a *sine qua non* in a democratic society. I am talking here about the practice of telegraphing policy actions well in advance. The effect of such a policy is to make investors feel more secure and safe: When they feel safer they take greater risks and use more leverage; when they use more leverage, the ultimate crack-up—when a central bank fails to control every aspect of the environment—is worse than it otherwise would have been. As I wrote in *Maestro, My Ass!*[1]:

> *Economic actors, in short, evolve their responses based on the environment. And, under Greenspan, it was clear that the environment was designed to always be sunny, safe, and warm. There was scant need for a margin of safety when nothing bad had ever happened and was never permitted to happen. Economic actors relaxed, because it was in their interest to do so. Why evolve a hardened shell, with all of the energy that requires, if you never need a hardened shell?*

But there always comes a time when the levees erected to keep us dry are breached. It is a fact of economic nature that there are (in Dr. Greenspan's terms on that October day) "once-in-a-century credit tsunamis." It is at those times that the heavy lifting of economic evolution occurs. The soundest entities survive. The risk is that if all of these entities have been evolving unsafe strategies, the resulting economic carnage can change the system forever.

The transparency ship, however, has sailed. I do not think that it will be easy to put that genie back in the bottle. Moreover, it isn't a theoretical failing. From a theory standpoint, the Fed is most likely correct that being transparent gives it more control over longer-term interest rates (aka "the rates that matter"), since longer-term interest rates are more likely to respond to information about the longer-term trajectory of Fed action than to one-off movements in overnight interest rates. It is just from a practical perspective that, perhaps, it may be the wrong thing to do.

The other major revolution in central banking, though, is much worse because I believe this is simply an error.

Although Friedman once said, "We are all Keynesians now,"[2] in point of fact by the late 1970s and early 1980s, the U.S. central bank was largely monetarist in philosophy. It wasn't that all of the economists in the world were monetarists, but more that the exceedingly good track record of monetarist predictions, augmented by a gifted spokesman in Milton Friedman, made monetarism the dominant theoretical framework that central bankers operated with. It was not necessarily a pure form of monetarism, but the basic philosophy that allowed the Volcker Fed to rein in inflation by reining in money growth, even though there were wrenching effects on the economy as a whole. But there can be no doubt about the Volcker policy—it was inspired by monetarism, and it succeeded famously in just the way theory predicted.

And this is why it is so flummoxing that in global central banking circles today, you can count the number of practicing and publishing monetarists on the fingers of one hand. One of the most vocal of these monetarists is Daniel Thornton, who retired from the Federal Reserve Bank of St. Louis in 2014. The St. Louis Fed, for a long time, had been the citadel of monetarism in central banking. Over the last few decades, the citadel has been overrun. In 2012, Dr. Thorton lamented in a short "Economic Synopses" publication of the St. Louis Fed, "...discussions of the money supply are *nearly nonexistent* in modern monetary theory and policy..."[3] (emphasis added), which is a tremendous change from the early 1980s, when the money supply was clearly the main variable the Fed aimed to manipulate in order to produce the macroeconomic outcomes it desired.

Even the manner in which central bankers talk and think about interest rates has changed. Notice the evolution in the way the FOMC communicates policy actions with respect to interest rates (one way in which transparency has helped is that it has made this evolution plain even to people outside the central bank):

In the implementation of policy for the immediate future, the Committee seeks to maintain the existing degree of pressure on reserve positions ... somewhat greater reserve restraint would, or slightly lesser reserve restraint might, be acceptable in the intermeeting period. The contemplated reserve conditions are expected to be consistent with growth of M2 and M3 over the period from December through March at annual rates of about 2 and 3½ percent, respectively.
—February, 1989 FOMC domestic policy directive.

Notice that the main focus in that statement is how pressure on reserves affects money supply growth. By 1994, the Fed was drawing the line to interest rates, rather than reserves, more explicitly. The press release following the February 4, 1994, meeting said in part:

> *Chairman Alan Greenspan announced today that the Federal Open Market Committee decided to increase slightly the degree of pressure on reserve positions. The action is expected to be associated with a small increase in short-term money market interest rates.*

The Federal Reserve eventually stopped talking about "reserve positions," although that continued to be how interest rates were managed in fact. Here is what the Fed was saying in January 2007:

> *The Federal Open Market Committee decided today to keep its target for the federal funds rate at 5$^1/_4$ percent.*

Today, of course, the Fed not only sets the current level of interest rates but also gives us an expected path of rates, even though we shouldn't care about rates from a policy perspective but only from a trading or investing perspective. As such, we appreciate the clarity but it is destructive, not constructive, to tie policy to rates.

But do not forget: Even when the Fed was talking about the interest rate target, the Fed actually managed interest rates by managing reserves. By doing large "system repos" or "matched sales," the supply of reserves was managed with respect to what the Fed thought the demand for reserves (which is unobservable in real time) was. If the resulting interest rate was too low or too high, then they added or subtracted to the supply of reserves. And thus we get to the point that is crucial for understanding how monetary policy is conducted: The interest rate is a measurement of the pressure on reserves, but what really matters is money. From within the Fed, Dr. Thornton was again a lone voice in the wilderness. In an October 2012 paper titled "Monetary Policy: Why Money Matters *and Interest Rates Don't*"[4] (emphasis in original), Thornton began confrontationally: "Today 'monetary policy' should more aptly be named 'interest rate policy' because policymakers pay virtually no attention to money."

So what happened over these last few decades? Remember, monetarists broke the back of the Great Inflation with a simple policy prescription. Monetarism explains the deflationary "trap" that Japan has been in for a few decades. Table 7.1 makes the argument plain. Why was Japan in a deflationary trap? Were the "lost decade(s)" due to demographics, as the popular belief has it?

On the contrary, the real surprise is that inflation in Japan didn't drop further, given the fact that average money growth dropped 6 percent per year after 1991. In fact, since the demographic challenges probably lowered the potential output of the country, it is more likely that the demographic effect prevented inflation from falling more than it did!

If the predictions of the theory have been so successful, why have the monetarists been routed from monetary policymaking? I believe is it because monetarism, compared to New Keynesian or other sorts of models, is simple. There is a conceit among

TABLE 7.1 **Japanese Money Growth and Inflation, 1980–2015**

	Average Annual M2 Growth	Average Annual CPI ex Fresh Food
1980–1991	8.9%	2.6%
1992–2015	2.5%	0.3%

Source: Japan Ministry of Internal Affairs and Communications; Bank of Japan; Economic and Social Research Institute Japan

professionals—in almost any profession—that if something is simple, it cannot be right. On Wall Street, for example, if you have a fancy, deeply quantitative valuation model that gives very precise values, then the risk management department is more likely to approve its use than if you have a simple model that is less precise, even if the simple model reflects a deeper understanding which is more likely to work in unusual "out of sample range" periods. Precision is confused with accuracy.

A cynic might further observe that very complex systems also serve as job security. Friedman advocated replacing the Fed with a computer that would simply maintain the money supply in line with the $MV \equiv PQ$ prescription. No one, to my knowledge, has considered replacing the Fed with a computer recently. Who would calculate the evolution of the Wicksellian equilibrium real interest rate and estimate the dynamic stochastic general equilibrium (DSGE) model? Who would publish all of the papers explaining why it didn't work and how the model needed to be reparameterized?

This is, sadly, no joke. Economic policymakers are almost uniformly academics, as opposed to practitioners, and academics like to develop theories—and the more complex, the better. Sometimes, reality is so complex that to fully model a phenomenon a very complex model is necessary. Think quantum physics. But even in these cases, a basic model can be more useful because it makes understanding of the primary issues easier. As George E. P. Box once wrote, "All models are wrong, but some models are useful."[5]

To be sure, developing competing models of a phenomenon is useful, but only if the models can be tested. In economics, we don't get to conduct controlled experiments. So, for example, during the late 1980s until the late 1990s everything that central bankers tried seemed to work—and this was taken as confirmation of the model. Growth was generally strong, especially late in the 1990s, with low inflation. This was the opposite of the stagflation of the 1970s, and even if the Fed did wrestle with the *jobless recovery* of the early 1990s, on the whole the economics profession felt that it had won, and the models that economists were using were working. It may be that another model would have prescribed similar actions, or that the economy would have experienced this golden decade if simply left alone, or that monetary policy was completely ineffective and this good outcome was the result of natural forces and trends. It should also be noted that the golden decade did not end well, so the victory laps that central bankers were taking—which produced book titles like *Maestro: Greenspan's Fed and the American Boom*[6] and magazine articles like *Fortune's* "In Greenspan We Trust"[7] or *Business Week's* "Alan Greenspan's Brave New World"—were, shall we say, premature.[8]

But by that time, monetarists had been fading, since they didn't publish as frequently or produce models as intricate as the New Keynesian models. The Fed, and other central banks, were primarily New Keynesians, and argued about parameter inputs or functional forms of the equations rather than about whether the models were just plain wrong.

And the failure to realize that their models were just plain wrong left them woefully unprepared when the Global Financial Crisis hit in 2007.

Notes

1. Michael Ashton, *Maestro, My Ass!* (Groundbreaking Press, 2009). Austin, TX.
2. In fact, Friedman's original statement was somewhat less shocking: "In one sense, we are all Keynesians now; in another, nobody is any longer a Keynesian."
3. Daniel L. Thornton, "Quantitative Easing and Money Growth: Potential for Higher Inflation," *Economic Synopses*, Federal Reserve Bank of St. Louis, February 3, 2012.

4. Daniel L. Thornton, "Monetary Policy: Why Money Matters *and Interest Rates Don't*," Working paper, Federal Reserve Bank of St. Louis Working Paper Series, #2012-020A, October 2012.
5. G. E. P. Box and N. R. Draper, *Empirical Model Building and Response Surfaces* (New York: John Wiley & Sons, 1987), p. 424.
6. Bob Woodward, *Maestro: Greenspan's Fed and the American Boom* (New York: Simon & Schuster, 2001).
7. Rob Norton, "In Greenspan We Trust," *Fortune* (March 18, 1996).
8. Dean Foust, "Alan Greenspan's Brave New World," *Business Week* (July 14, 1997).

CHAPTER 8

Central Bankers in the Global Financial Crisis

In the last chapter, I discussed the devolution of central banking over the last three decades. In this chapter, I will address the actions of central bankers leading up to, during, and after the Global Financial Crisis of 2007–2009. Before I do, though, I want to recall why we care so much about central bankers.

This book is about what's wrong with money. Central bankers are the stewards of money. They may not be stewards of the currency, or of the exchange rate; however, in protecting and perpetuating the "system" and in their actions in support of the goal to keep inflation low (thus maintaining the purchasing power of money), they really are protecting confidence in money itself. It is no accident that the interbank payment systems go through the Fed, and that the first calls between the Fed and banks after 9/11 were about the fund transfer system being "fully operational." If it is the train dispatcher's job to keep the trains running on time, it is the central bank's job to make the money run on time.

We care about central bankers the same way we care about the train dispatcher: If they mess up, it can cause an awful mess. The value of money relies on confidence, so it is crucial that the money stewards inspire confidence.

Central Banking before the Crisis

In the lead-up to the Global Financial Crisis, monetary policy made mistakes but they were the normal kind of mistakes. Although the Fed is the largest single employer of PhD economists in the world, their joint forecasts are no more accurate (and often less accurate) than those of private forecasters even though they have inside information about the most likely course of monetary policy!

The financial crisis really started about 18 months before Lehman collapsed on September 15, 2008. Early in 2007, strains in the subprime mortgage market became obvious to people close to that market, although Fed Chairman Ben Bernanke testified in March 2007 that "the impact on the broader economy and financial markets of the problems in the subprime market seems likely to be contained." By the summer of 2007, the problems were widely realized as Bear Stearns first offered to bail out one of its structured credit funds (in June), and then in mid-July disclosed that two hedge funds that trafficked in subprime mortgages had been essentially wiped out.

This was a huge deal and was added to widespread signs that the U.S. economy as a whole was peaking. For example, housing starts had long since peaked—in early 2006—at a rate of more than 2.2 million units per year; by mid-2007 that figure was 1.4 million, the slowest pace of home starts in a decade. The Fed funds rate stood at $5\frac{1}{4}\%$. Core inflation had declined from 3% to a mere 2.2%.

What is the correct central bank response here? It is never incorrect to say "do nothing," if philosophically you want to run a passive central bank that merely focuses on keeping a steady hand on the tiller. In fact, the FOMC did nothing. But (and this may seem very picky) the Committee did nothing for the wrong reasons. It wasn't that it believed a central bank should merely police the soundness of major financial institutions—which at the time there was little reason yet to question—and maintain a steady flow of money. The statement released at the conclusion of the August 7, 2007, FOMC meeting read (emphasis added):

> *The Federal Open Market Committee decided today to keep its target for the federal funds rate at 5¹/₄ percent.*
>
> *Economic growth was moderate during the first half of the year. Financial markets have been volatile in recent weeks, credit conditions have become tighter for some households and businesses, and the housing correction is ongoing. Nevertheless, the economy seems likely to continue to expand at a moderate pace over coming quarters, **supported by solid growth in employment and incomes and a robust global economy**.*
>
> *Readings on core inflation have improved modestly in recent months. However, a sustained moderation in inflation pressures has yet to be convincingly demonstrated. **Moreover, the high level of resource utilization has the potential to sustain those pressures**.*
>
> *Although the downside risks to growth have increased somewhat, the Committee's predominant policy concern remains the risk that inflation will fail to moderate as expected. Future policy adjustments will depend on the outlook for both inflation and economic growth, as implied by incoming information.*

The Fed, which was ideally positioned to see the developing pressures, looked backwards at the "robust global economy" and remained concerned about inflation based on a New Keynesian model even though core inflation had been ebbing for a year and M2 money growth was around 6.5 percent—too high for truly stable prices, but hardly alarming.

It bears noting that although the Fed fiddled, the European Central Bank responded to tightening conditions in the overnight money markets—a sign of systemic stress—by offering to lend aggressively at the ECB's stated target rate. Banks took around €100 billion in the initial ECB operation. The Fed took note of this, and on August 10 (three days after it stood pat and issued the previous statement after its regular meeting) felt it necessary to issue this new statement:

> *The Federal Reserve will provide reserves as necessary through open market operations to promote trading in the federal funds market at rates close to the Federal Open Market Committee's target rate of 5¹/₄ percent. In current circumstances, depository institutions may experience unusual funding needs because of dislocations in money and credit markets. As always, the discount window is available as a source of funding.*

One week later, the Federal Reserve cut the discount rate by 50 bps at an unscheduled (aka "emergency") meeting, saying, "Downside risks to growth have increased appreciably." The FOMC subsequently began to move the Fed funds rate lower as well.

The general theme of central banking at the front end of the crisis was "too little, too late." But that, as I said, is a normal sort of central banking error. Central banks are almost always late, and they almost never calibrate policy correctly. We are satisfied when they are close, when the metaphorical train is only a few minutes late.

Central Banking during the Crisis

But as the crisis deepened, the normal tools seemed to not be working (if, by "working," we mean that somehow extra liquidity could restore growth to an economy that had overbuilt and was experiencing a classic unwind of asset prices driven to bubble-like levels). The Fed began to invent new tools. The first of these tools was the Term Auction Facility (TAF) in December 2007, via which the Fed would offer term loans to banks that could be backed by a wide variety of collateral.

In March 2008, the Fed introduced the Term Securities Lending Facility (TSLF), which lent Treasuries in exchange for other less-liquid securities; the idea was that banks had plenty of good bonds, but these bonds weren't being accepted as collateral in the interbank markets so the Fed agreed to lend them securities that they *could* lend in the interbank market. I should point out that lending securities against cash in the interbank market is a very important function in the banking system. If a bank needs to spend $100 to buy a $100 bond, then it cannot also lend that $100 to someone seeking a loan and the cost to be a market-maker in such a bond is greatly increased in terms of both capital requirements and opportunity costs. So more typically a bank might borrow, say, $90 of the value of the $100 bond, using the bond as collateral, freeing up that capital for lending or market-making or other activities. If a bank cannot borrow the $90, or in general cannot borrow against many of the securities it holds, then it must sell those bonds in a *fire-sale* transaction. So the Fed, via the TSLF, believed that it was promoting the healthy functioning of interbank lending markets.

Five days later, the Fed also established the Primary Dealer Credit Facility (PDCF), by which it extended the credit directly to dealers against their securities portfolios. It was seemingly intended to help Bear Stearns, which had been shut out of the markets, but it was too late: That same day, Bear Stearns agreed to be bought by JPMorgan Chase at a price of $2/share (speaking of fire sales), to avoid filing Chapter 7.

These were challenging times, although to this point in the story the damage from the imploding mortgage market still appeared "contained" to impact mainly financial institutions.

The stock market only entered a technical bear market in July of 2008, down more than 20 percent from the highs, but panic was distinctly absent. The economy was clearly weakening, but since the unemployment rate had been a sterling 4.4 percent in 2006, the rise in mid-2008 to 5.6 percent was something less than cataclysmic. But in the late summer of 2008, that all changed. In June, Bank of America acquired Countrywide Financial, to save the mortgage lender from a messy denouement. In July, the Office of Thrift Supervision closed IndyMac Bank, one of the largest bank closures to that point, and the Securities Exchange Commission (SEC) temporarily prohibited short-selling the stocks and bonds of Fannie Mae and Freddie Mac, as well as the stocks of primary dealers.

In September, the crisis began to rise to a crescendo. Fannie Mae and Freddie Mac were placed in government conservatorship on September 7. But the crucial act was the bankruptcy of Lehman Brothers.

Lehman had been fighting off the dogs for some days. The company's ability to transact in the derivatives markets, which at the time were largely bilateral (meaning that Bank X faced Bank Y, directly, without going through a clearinghouse) and required credit lines established from each firm to the other, was already seriously impaired as the week of September 8 began. Some banks had "pulled their lines" to Lehman, meaning that their credit departments would not approve any new swaps with that firm but only unwinds of existing deals. But traders (including the author) were very sensitive about publicly refusing Lehman's credit in the interbank market.

Typically (in the days before a clearinghouse was set up to be the counterparty for all trades), a trader would act on a price shown by a broker, and then find out who his or her counterparty would be, following something like this script:

Interbank Broker:	I am 23 offered for five hundred million.
Trader:	Mine. I pay 23 in five hundred. What name am I checking?
Interbank Broker:	Check Barclays Bank PLC–London. Who are you?
Trader:	I am Natixis FP–Paris.
Interbank Broker (after a pause):	He is good to you.[1]
Trader (after a pause):	I can do Barclays. Done.
Interbank Broker:	Done. Are you free for dinner?

The trade would then be reported to the market in terms of the price, tenor, and size, although the names of the bank trading counterparties were supposed to be confidential. This procedure worked in this fashion for 95 percent of all transactions. Of the remaining 5 percent, some minor adjustment needed to be negotiated. Perhaps the Barclays trader could deal with Natixis's New York branch, but didn't have a line to the Paris branch, or maybe the Natixis trader needed to get his credit department to approve the line for $500 million because he was "full" on the Barclays name—getting an increase to the credit limit just like you can do with your credit card company, if you're about to make a big purchase but have good credit overall. These are common and simple adjustments.

Sometimes, Bank A would be full on Bank B's name and unable to complete the trade, or wouldn't have lines at all if B was a small bank that didn't deal in the interbank market very often. Again, ordinarily this wasn't a big problem because another bank would step in and complete the trade. However, it was very rare for the big derivatives dealers like Morgan Stanley, Goldman Sachs, JP Morgan, Lehman Brothers, Barclays, and so on to decline one another's names.

During the week of September 8, though, market participants realized that the situation was significantly different. No one wanted to be the bank that declined Lehman's name publicly and started a panic. The next step would have been a rumor getting to CNBC and there would be no saving the firm then. Traders quietly told their brokers "Don't show me Lehman," meaning that "if there's a 23 offer but it is from Lehman, don't tell me because I don't want to lift the price and have to decline Lehman's credit publicly." This was a bad situation, and clearly something had to happen. While the rest of America watched the real economy sputter, Wall Street dealers braced for the worst.

And on September 15, 2008, the worst is exactly what they got.

The collapse of Lehman Brothers has been documented extensively elsewhere, and I won't retell that tale here. What is worth documenting is the effect of the failure on the operation of the financial markets and the behavior of the Federal Reserve before and after the Lehman debacle.

September 15, 2008, marked an inflection point. Prior to Lehman, the Federal Reserve had been acting in a typical provision-of-liquidity role, both by increasing interbank reserves (lowering interest rates as an effect of that action) and by facilitating the substitution of good collateral for impaired (but still valuable) collateral, making the continued financing of bank balance sheets and trading books feasible. By the time of Lehman's failure, however, conventional tools (and unconventional extensions of conventional tools) had been largely exhausted. And the markets were seizing up.

It is hard to overstate the gravity of the situation in the banking community in September 2008. I remember the period clearly. I worked at the time as the inflation derivatives trader at the U.S. branch of a large foreign bank that, only two years previously, had held the top rating from all of the ratings agencies. Each morning during the crisis, I would walk over to the

Treasury desk, whose function was to borrow money against the bank's portfolio of securities or borrow money unsecured against our general credit in the marketplace. During normal times, the specialists who ply their trade in this crucial function work hard to finance the bank at the best overall rate possible, and they are done with the heavy lifting fairly early in the morning (early in the New York morning is when the best money-market liquidity is found, as European banks are still dealing). When I walked over to the Treasury desk, I would ask a simple and yet profoundly important question: "How are we doing? Do we have the bank funded yet?"

This was a great way to measure the progress of the bank funding part of the crisis, which was, after all, the most dangerous part. For, whether you care for bankers or not, a system that is without banks—and even worse, suddenly without banks—is not one where money is likely to be well-respected and secure.

If we were having trouble funding our balance sheet, then I knew everyone else was as well. And while the answer from our desk was always, "We got it done," sometimes that answer didn't come until after lunch, or not until we had borrowed billions of dollars at a usurious overnight rate from our parent company. The stress on that desk was palpable—because failure to fund the bank would mean we might well follow Lehman in seeking the protection of the bankruptcy courts.

As the panic progressed, the terms of the money we were able to borrow worsened. First there was no more six-month money, then no three-month money, and finally no one would lend for any period longer than overnight. The commercial paper market, where banks and large corporations can borrow unsecured money from money-market mutual funds and other investors trying to earn a few incremental basis points of extra return on their cash, began to dry up as well. Investors, wary of being an unsecured creditor to a bank—any bank—stopped rolling over maturing commercial paper. This was no idle fear:

On September 16th, the Reserve Primary Money Fund "broke the buck" with its net asset value falling below $1 per share, thanks to losses on Lehman commercial paper, and no "ultra safe" money fund wanted to be next. It was bad. Every day, I braced myself for the news from the desk that "we might not get it done today."

During this time, the Fed shifted gears. A cynic might say that it stripped the gears, as it rolled out one program after another. Unlike the pre-Lehman programs, these post-Lehman programs involved the Fed in actively guaranteeing assets, which is clearly beyond the legislatively contemplated role of that institution:

- On September 16, the Federal Reserve Bank of New York was authorized by the Federal Reserve Board to lend up to $85 billion to AIG, which was not a banking institution, in exchange for an 80 percent equity interest in the firm. This had the effect of guaranteeing the swaps that AIG was a party to.
- On September 19, the Fed announced the creation of the Asset-Backed Commercial Paper Money Market Mutual Fund Liquidity Facility (AMLF, presumably because ABCPMMM-FLF was absurdly long), which made nonrecourse loans to banks so that the banks could buy asset-backed commercial paper from money market mutual funds without any real risk—helping the money-market funds get some liquidity back.
- On October 7, the Fed announced the Commercial Paper Funding Facility (CPFF), which created a special-purpose vehicle to buy commercial paper directly from issuers (such as banks). Remember that commercial paper is unsecured.
- On November 23, the Fed agreed to backstop residual risk in a $306 billion pool of commercial and residential mortgage-backed securities held by Citigroup, in exchange

for preferred shares issued to the Treasury and FDIC. (On January 16, the Fed offered a similar deal to Bank of America on a $118 billion portfolio.)

- On November 25, the Fed announced the creation of the Term Asset-Backed Securities Lending Facility (TALF), which made nonrecourse loans to holders of highly rated asset-backed securities and recent consumer and small business loans.

Other agencies of the government were also heavily involved: Congress created the Troubled Asset Relief Program (TARP), the Treasury bought $125 billion of preferred stock in nine banks, and the FDIC created the Temporary Liquidity Guarantee Program (TLGP) to guarantee the senior debt of FDIC-insured banks. But the Treasury and the FDIC are equipped—and, more importantly, authorized—to make such dramatic gestures. It is fairly clear that the Fed at least tiptoed across the boundaries of its mandate, and may have leapt across them.

But it also is hard to fault the Federal Reserve Board of Governors for trying to push the envelope. While I personally believe that we would be better off today if free market forces had been allowed to cull a few more weak derivatives dealers, there is no doubt that at the time that was a difficult position to take. After all, policymakers allowed Lehman to fail completely, and also witnessed the extinction of Bear Stearns. Surely those two events ought to be enough to make the "moral hazard" point that poorly run institutions will not automatically be bailed out. In any event, circumstances at the time were extremely scary—and the Fed, after all, is tasked with the safety and soundness of the financial system. If occasionally it trods slightly on the wrong side of technical legality, it can be forgiven that trespass. In the end, the Fed's frenetic acronym creation worked. On the day the

Commercial Paper Funding Facility went into effect, my trip to the Treasury desk was met with "Oh, we're fine. No troubles today." The repeated application of the cardiac paddles had worked. "Clear!" Zap! The interbank funding markets were working again.

It is what happened *next* where the Fed made the big mistakes.

Central Banking after the Crisis

By late October, although the worst was behind us in terms of the stability of the banking system, the worst was clearly yet ahead in the performance of the economy. The implosion of the housing market, with all of the leveraged "investors" who were suddenly bankrupt, ensured that that mortgage-backed securities market would be a mess for a while. Homeowners who suddenly found themselves deep underwater in their loan-to-value also were clearly at greater risk to default on their mortgages. The term *jingle mail* entered the popular lexicon. Jingle mail is when a homeowner who owes far more on his or her house than it is worth defaults by mailing the house keys to the lender. "Take it, it's yours." While this probably didn't literally happen all that often, the point of the phrase is that at some level defaulting on a mortgage arguably becomes an economically rational thing to do. Figure 8.1 shows that the delinquency rate on single-family residential mortgages by early 2010 had risen to *seven times* its pre-crisis level.

Of course, the collapse of housing also meant that many jobs were lost in construction and in a number of other ancillary trades. Although it took the National Bureau of Economic Research until December 2008 to declare that a recession had begun one year earlier, the recession was plain to see for most everyone by the middle of that year. The seizing up of financial

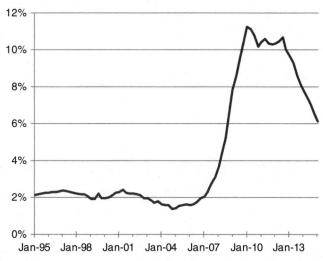

FIGURE 8.1 **Delinquency rate on single-family residential mortgages, booked in domestic offices, all commercial banks**
Source: Board of Governors of the Federal Reserve System (US)

markets caused bank credit to decline. After adjusting the data for the fact that Goldman Sachs and Morgan Stanley suddenly decided to become banks in the middle of the crisis, bank credit dropped about 8 percent—nearly $1 trillion—between October 2008 and May 2010. The question was whether we would get a "garden-variety" recession of, say, 3 to 5 percent of GDP, or something Depression-like of 10 to 20 percent of GDP.

And so, of course, the Federal Reserve rode to the rescue again.

Before we continue this story, let me harken back to Chapter 3 and the power of monetary policy. This is a good point at which to recall that "with these tools, in the absence of money illusion, the only thing a central bank can really accomplish, as Figure 3.1 showed, is to target the price level over time...What a central bank cannot do is to energize real growth." However, since monetarists are in sharp retreat at the Federal Reserve and all other central banks, this fact (despite the voluminous empirical evidence in support of this proposition) apparently carried no weight in deliberations.

On November 25, 2008, the Fed announced its first "quantitative easing" (QE) measure, although it was couched in terms of credit provision. The central bank announced that it would purchase up to $100 billion of direct obligations of housing-related government-sponsored enterprises (GSEs) such as Fannie Mae, Freddie Mac, and the Federal Home Loan Banks. Additionally, it would purchase up to $500 billion in mortgage-backed securities (MBSs) issued by Fannie, Freddie, and Ginnie Mae. The stated purpose of these purchases was to help lower interest rates in the mortgage markets, which it succeeded in doing. But the problems in housing had nothing to do with interest rates and everything to do with housing prices. If home prices are going to fall 10 percent, then financing the purchase of a home with a mortgage that is 5 percent rather than 6 percent is not likely to affect your purchase decision.

In March 2009, the Fed upped the ante by declaring its intention to buy $300 billion in longer-term Treasuries, plus another $750 billion of MBS and another $100 billion of GSE debt. For those keeping score at home, this means that by the end of these programs the Fed had bought $1.75 billion in securities. This was "QE1," although we didn't know at the time that this was only the first round of quantitative easing (just as World War I was simply called the "Great War" until there was a second one). The Bank of England also began to buy assets in a quantitative-easing program, in roughly the same scale (relative to UK GDP) as the Fed's action: £200 billion. The European Central Bank (ECB) started the purchase of €60 billion of covered bonds in May 2009. Collectively, these were called "Large Scale Asset Purchases," or LSAPs by the acronym-loving central bankers.

After pausing for a couple of months in 2010, the Fed started to worry about deflation since core inflation was steadily declining—eventually hitting 0.6 percent in October 2010.

This was an unhealthy focus on numbers, rather than understanding: Core inflation was so low because housing prices had plummeted and eventually pulled rents lower. Rent of primary residence (that is, if you live in an apartment, for example), plus the imputed rent of homes that are owned and lived in, constitutes a very large chunk of consumer expenditures and, thus, a large chunk of inflation indices such as the Consumer Price Index. But despite the housing crisis, and despite the sharp recession, and confounding all of the forecasts of Keynesian economists, prices other than housing prices were still rising at 1 to 2 percent a year. Figure 8.2 illustrates the complete failure of Keynesian prediction: Given the deepest recession since the Great Depression, Keynesian economists expected prices to decline outright and thus feared deflation. As the figure illustrates, however, inflation outside of food and energy barely even slowed.

With this fear of deflation haunting every decision, the Fed tossed another log on the fire by announcing what became

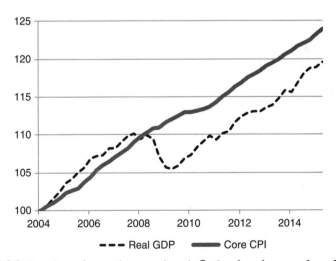

FIGURE 8.2 **Despite a dramatic recession, inflation barely even slowed, in sharp contrast to Keynesian predictions.**
Source: Bureau of Labor Statistics, Bureau of Economic Analysis

known as "QE2": another $600 billion of Treasury purchases. The switch to buying only Treasury securities came as the central bank began to be concerned that its purchases of MBS were affecting liquidity in that market, but it also concerned monetary policy watchdogs since it looked an awful lot like "monetizing the debt."

When a government is in real trouble, it sometimes resorts to printing money—in the old days, like with old Kublai Khan back in Chapter 5, it would print actual money; today, of course, we don't need the printing press to accomplish the same thing electronically. But this almost always leads to a collapse of the currency, since ever-larger quantities of money are set against the same amount of societal resources. But there is a sneakier way to accomplish the same thing, and that is for the government to borrow money, issuing bonds to represent the debt, and then to have the central bank exchange the debt for money, and thereafter retire the debt. In that case, the government need never pay back the debt, and the money remains in circulation. It is the same as printing money, in the end.

Of course, the sneaky bit is that we don't know whether the debt has been monetized until after the debt matures. If the debt matures while the central bank is holding the bonds, then monetization has been accomplished. If the debt is sold back into the market prior to maturity, then the transaction has been reversed and no monetization has occurred.

Once QE2 ended, the Fed—still trying to get the economy growing and no longer concerned about bank liquidity—began a swap of the shorter-term Treasuries it held for longer-term Treasuries in the market, with the intention of lowering longer-term rates. When this program was also ineffective at generating robust economic growth, the FOMC in late 2012 introduced "QE3," popularly called QE∞ or QE-infinity because it was open-ended. In this latter program, the Fed pledged to buy $40 billion in MBS (and then later added

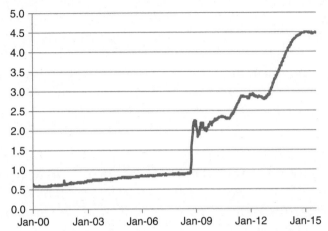

FIGURE 8.3 Total assets of the Federal Reserve, trillions of dollars
Source: Federal Reserve

$45 billion of Treasuries) per month, every month, with no end date determined. When QE3 finally ended in 2014, the Fed's balance sheet held nearly $4.5 trillion in assets, about 4.5 times its size in mid-2008 (see Figure 8.3). All of that quantitative easing had managed to produce GDP growth averaging a whopping 2.0 percent for the 16 quarters of 2011–2014.

Of course, we can never know for sure what would have happened to the economy had central banks not embarked on the unprecedented large-scale asset purchase programs. Keynesians argue that we would have been much worse off had the Fed not done the large-scale asset purchases. Some true believers such as Nobel Laureate Paul Krugman argued that QE was simply too small; in 2010, he argued that something on the order of $8–10 trillion was the right figure.

But the flip side of buying $3.5 trillion in securities, of course, was that the Fed had injected $3.5 trillion into the U.S. financial system. This caused much consternation in certain quarters. If $850 billion in "base money" (currency, plus bank reserves, which are the flip side of the Fed's balance sheet) suddenly became five times that amount, the fear was that inflation, even hyperinflation, would soon follow per the $MV \equiv PQ$ relationship.

These predictions give monetarism a bad name. Bank reserves are not money: No one spends reserves. They are not a medium of exchange; they are not part of the transactional money supply. Bank reserves, however, support the creation of money through the multiplier effect of fractional reserve banking: If each dollar of reserves becomes ten dollars of money via bank loans, then we can focus on base money as being the important metric. But the problem is that the people who focused on base money were overlooking their crucial assumption—the assumption that the multiplier would be stable, that every dollar of reserves would become some number of dollars of M2, no matter how fast or how large bank reserves grew.

We don't care about base money. We care about M2 and other measures of money supply that can be spent. And in the crisis, the Fed—intentionally or unintentionally—created a very effective mechanism to sunder the connection between the massive injection of bank reserves and the creation of money.

The Fed paid banks to refrain from lending.

During the crisis, the Fed began for the first time to pay "interest on excess reserves" (IOER) to banks. It did this in order to keep overnight interest rates from declining too much. Ordinarily, when a bank has too many reserves, it lends them in the interbank market to other banks that are short a bit. Before the Federal Reserve paid interest on excess reserves, banks would have lent their excess reserves at any rate, down to a tiny sliver above zero percent, because otherwise the reserves would earn exactly zero. Since the entire system had far too many reserves, this is exactly what would have happened. But the Fed didn't want interest rates that low, because it was concerned about whether money-market funds could survive if interest rates were zero and it didn't want to destroy that part of the market. So the Fed started paying banks on their excess reserves. This was money for nothing as far as the banks were concerned, and especially with credit quality in general being sketchy during the crisis, it was easier to sit back and hold the excess reserves than to make loans that, while more profitable on a gross basis, also held the potential to add to the large pile of nonperforming loans the banks already had.

It was as if the Federal Reserve had shipped a large box of dollar bills to every bank, and then paid the banks to keep the boxes nailed shut and stored away in the vault. I think we can all see that, in such a circumstance, the reserves (boxes of currency) would not be money in the sense that they circulated in commerce. Put another way: If the currency in the boxes was never spent, then how could it possibly affect prices? It is as if the reserves never existed.

There are only a few niggling details that might matter, or might not, in the end.

The first detail is that no one knows how long banks will refrain from taking the tops off the boxes. During the crisis, with credit quality weak and banks risk-averse, it didn't take much persuasion to keep banks from lending. But will that always be true? Banks are still somewhat capital constrained, in that there is only so much credit they can extend on a given base of capital, and that capital was weakened in the crisis. But at some point, as banks get stronger, some of those reserves will start to be lent. And we don't know how that will happen, because no one has ever done this before with $100 billion, much less $3.5 trillion.

The second detail is that the Fed has not been able to formulate a plan for how to call those boxes back when they are no longer needed, or when they notice that banks are starting to open them. I will talk more about this in the next chapter, and the implication it has for central bank potency.

Keynesians, and this includes most central bankers, have had a good laugh at the monetarists. The fact that the mainstream Keynesian prediction of deflation was in horrible error was set against the prediction of fringe "monetarists" that hyperinflation was going to set in. But the mainstream monetarists never made such predictions because we focused on money, not reserves.

The failure of the quantitative easing to produce immediate inflation seemed to argue for more quantitative easing. And why not? If there are no negative consequences to money printing—and Keynesians from Krugman to the current denizens of central banking policy circles see none—then why not keep buying up securities and pumping in reserves? At the very least, banks have been forcibly delevered, as they now have far more reserves than they can use. And if there is even an incremental growth benefit to QE, perhaps on the argument that lower interest rates spur growth, then why shouldn't central banks keep on doing large-scale asset purchases? It's a perpetual motion machine—all benefits, no costs.

Forget about economics; try common sense. If this works, then why shouldn't the Fed keep doing it forever? And why hasn't the Fed ever done it before?

The answer, of course, is that the policy has not yet come full circle. And until it does, it is far too early for a victory lap. There are some reasons to think that the most difficult part of the Fed's job still lies ahead.

Note

1. This conversation is structurally identical to the sort of conversation that occurs every day between the derivatives desk of a major bank and the broker who facilitates transactions in the broker market between banks. It contains some shorthand phrasing. "I pay 23 in five hundred" tells the broker what price I want to pay, and for how much; because the trader is paying a price that was offered, he or she next asks for the official name of the counterparty ("What name am I checking?"). It is important

that the trader checks with the credit department either online or in person to make sure that there is legal documentation for this relationship and a sufficient amount left on the credit limit to be able to complete the transaction. The broker facilitates this exchange of information and then says "He is good to you," which means that the counterparty documentation and credit limits are satisfactory to complete the trade. "I can do Barclays" is another way of saying the same thing. Both sides having now confirmed the essential details, they say "done" as a sort of verbal handshake completing the trade.

CHAPTER 9

Where Are We Now?

There is the old story about the optimist who falls off the roof of a very tall building and, as he passes the seventh floor on his way down says, "So far, so good!"

Now, we all know that even great optimism cannot survive impact with the pavement. So this chapter is all about where the pavement is. The unfortunate, but realistic answer is that we haven't hit the pavement yet. The optimistic economist, investor, or analyst says "so far, so good" when it comes to the ministrations of global central banks, because we haven't yet had the crack-up. But unless we have completed the trip, we cannot know for sure what the consequences are of falling off that building (or, in the current circumstances, of jumping off of it). Similarly, until we have returned financial conditions to something near "neutral" or "normal," or established that it isn't necessary to ever do so, we cannot know the true cost of quantitative easing policy, nor if the monetarists are right about the impotence of monetary policy to affect real variables in the long run.

It should be noted that some of this optimism stems from the assumption that in order for interest rates to be normalized, they will need to rise. A strong assumption of current economic thinking is that rising interest rates dampen inflation; therefore, if inflation has not yet risen by the time that interest rates begin to rise, there will be no inflation and the only risk is growth. I think that is an incorrect conclusion, and I will explain why in this chapter. I will also present some of the other obstacles that stand between the current circumstance and policy neutrality, and hypothesize about some of the ways the situation may play out.

Of course, I don't know what is going to happen. The only difference between me and most of the economic (and policy) establishments is that I will admit it. One of the biggest problems we face today—which we did not face until the Fed began quantitative easing, after the crisis was essentially over—is that we have never done anything like this before. There is no precedent for quantitative easing of this magnitude. Central bankers rely on carefully formulated mathematical models that amount to just so much intellectual flatulence because we are not on a part of the chart where past history has a whole lot of useful information for us, or for these models.

I will say this: It is really hard to unscramble an egg, and our monetary system right now is well and thoroughly scrambled. I think there is an economic counterpart to the Second Law of Thermodynamics, which implies that in order to return a disorderly system back to its orderly state, you have to put more energy back into the system than it originally released. So, for example, if you break a glass it takes more energy to put the glass back together than the breaking of the glass released originally. My intuition is that economic systems work the same way. Earlier, I alluded to the notion of a "perpetual motion machine" in large-scale asset purchases, and this is the same concept. If a central bank can dramatically ease financial conditions—say, by buying a couple trillion dollars' worth of bonds, and then get back to neutral by selling those bonds and have the economy net improved—then they should do that all the time. Buy a trillion, sell a trillion, buy a trillion, sell a trillion, and sooner or later we will all be hopelessly rich. That would be the economic equivalent to the sort of transaction with energy that the Second Law of Thermodynamics prohibits.

But I rather suspect that in doing the round trip, things end up somewhat worse off. The other implication of the Second Law is that the amount of net energy required to get the system back to the original state increases as the system gets less efficient. And with the economic parallel, I must say that the connection between the world of money and the world of real goods is very inefficient. If it were efficient, then central banking would be much easier, like operating an engine. While I think that central banks in the crisis made some very large mistakes, I must also say that even a perfectly run central bank leaves lots of wiggle in the economy because there is a fundamental quantum of randomness in economic life—which makes me think of quantum mechanics.

Never mind. The point I am making is that, absent a return to something approximating the economy's original monetary state—with interest rates at neutral levels, the Fed's balance sheet at something like the old levels, and so on—it is utterly irresponsible to call monetary policy from 2008 to the present a success. And yet, as early as January 2011 Janet Yellen, who was then vice-chair of the Fed, issued a stirring defense of the LSAP program.[1] In a nutshell, Dr. Yellen's argument in that speech boiled down to this:

- The LSAP program is not affecting the dollar.
- The LSAP program is not triggering "significant excesses or imbalances in the United States."
- The LSAP program does not risk markedly higher inflation because there is slack in the economy.
- However, the LSAP program has had an enormous effect on jobs, adding about 3 million jobs to the economy.

Ergo, the program has been hugely successful in the ways they needed it to be, without any side effects and no chance of anything going wrong. Does it make me a bad person that I am naturally suspicious of a drug that will make me immensely strong, lengthen my life, improve my love life, and cure hang-overs but has no negative side effects? How about if that drug worked as intended the first time it was tested?

I can't seem to escape physics at the moment, so I will quote the famous theoretical physicist Rudolf Pauli, who once reportedly remarked about an argument, "That's not right. It's not even wrong." The result of the monetary policy experiment conducted by the Federal Reserve and other central banks after 2008 has not been determined yet.

However, I think that we can probably see far enough to realize that the likely net result is unlikely to make us better off.

Excess Reserves Are Potential Energy—A Lot of It

At the end of Chapter 8, I presented an analogy for the effect those large-scale asset purchases had on the assets of banks, and why it was not very surprising that the great increase in the size of Federal Reserve liabilities had not led (at least yet) to inflation. If you think of the "excess reserves" that the Fed created as being crates of currency that the Fed was paying banks to keep shut, then it is obvious that this money is in no way affecting actual economic transactions in the economy. But here we are concerned with what happens next to those boxes. Should we care? Well, Figure 9.1 shows the relative sizes of the "excess" and "required" reserves buckets in the U.S. banking system as a whole.

Banks are absolutely crammed full with boxes of money. Of the $2.6 trillion in reserves held by banks, $2.45 trillion or so is "excess."

Why do we care? We care because of the meanings of *required* and *excess*. Required reserves are reserves (cash, or deposits held at the Fed) that the bank is required to hold against loans that they have made and other risky assets that they own. In the days before there were excess reserves in the

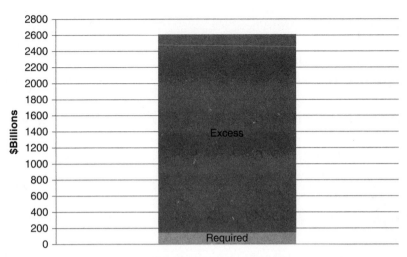

FIGURE 9.1 **Excess reserves of banks completely swamp required reserves.**
Source: Board of Governors of the Federal Reserve System (US)

system, the Federal Reserve controlled the money supply by increasing or decreasing the total amount of reserves in the system. If the total reserves declined, then banks had to curtail lending; if total reserves increased, then banks could expand lending (which they want to do, as long as opportunities for profitable lending are available, because they make money by lending) by acquiring and holding more of those reserves.

Excess reserves are just what they sound like: They are in excess of what banks need to hold.

Now, consider how monetary policy is implemented in this sort of circumstance. Suppose that the Fed wishes to restrain the growth of transactional money (M2, for example) in order to cool off economic growth. How do they do this?

The traditional option is that the Fed raises the overnight rate. The Fed announces this move, but the important part is what happens next: The Open Market Desk (aka, the Desk) conducts reverse repos to decrease the supply of reserves, or sells securities outright from the System Open Market Account (SOMA) if it wishes to make a more permanent adjustment.

This causes the price of reserves (also known as the overnight interest rate) to rise, and the Desk adjusts its activity so that the overnight rate floats near the target rate.

The problem is that this won't work right now. There are far too many reserves in circulation for the overnight interest rate to be increased by reverse repos or small securities sales. In fact, if it wasn't for the interest being paid on excess reserves, the overnight rate would certainly be zero, and might even be negative because the supply of reserves greatly outweighs the demand for reserves. They are called "excess" reserves for a reason—the bank doesn't need them, and will lend them overnight for pretty much any available rate.

So in order for the Fed to push the overnight rate higher by traditional methods of reverse repos or securities sales, it must first soak up all of the excess reserves in the system by selling bonds. Otherwise, any adjustment it makes will come from banks' excess reserves; accordingly, the Fed has no control over the quantity of loans that would be made in this circumstance. To be clear: Currently, monetary policy is impotent to control money.

The Federal Reserve is completely aware of this, which is why it has floated a number of trial balloons concerning ways it could drain all of those excess reserves efficiently. And it has come, grudgingly, to the conclusion that draining these excess reserves might not be as easy as it has claimed in the past. The pattern has been clear and should have been discomfiting. Here are some approaches that have been considered and discarded.

Plan A: Selling SOMA Securities

At first, the Fed thought to unwind the massive purchases of Treasuries by simply selling them. The original argument, made by the head of the Fed's Open Market Desk in a speech in March 2010,[2] was that the Fed pushed rates lower by buying

Treasuries, but selling them wouldn't raise interest rates. There are two problems with the idea of selling the massive bond position into the market.

The first problem is that when the Fed was buying its trillions, it was lucky enough to be facing a seller of trillions, also known as the U.S. Treasury. It worked out okay, because the Fed needed to buy what the Treasury was selling (not directly, of course, but the Fed was soaking up a lot of that paper). But now, if the Open Market Desk were to try and sell a couple of trillions of dollars' worth of bonds, they would find that the Treasury is also (still) selling about a half-trillion of new debt per year. While the Fed was doing LSAP, the seesaw was balanced; but now both big kids want to sit on the same side of the seesaw, and that isn't going to work.

The second problem with this approach is that if the Treasury started to unwind the SOMA portfolio securities and interest rates rise while it is doing so (and it would be really remarkable if they did not), then it is actually possible that it could sell all of the securities and still not drain all of the reserves, since the average selling price on the way down would most likely be lower than the average purchase price had been. That means the Fed would take in less money (draining it from the economy) than it put into the economy when it was making the initial purchases.

Plan B: Let SOMA Securities Mature

The Fed then thought it might just allow the securities in the SOMA to gradually roll off as they came due—that is, instead of reinvesting the proceeds in new bonds, the Fed would just keep the money. There are at least two problems with this plan. The theoretical problem is that this (eventually) solves the problem of the Fed's balance sheet being too large, but it doesn't reduce reserves—the Fed isn't removing money from the system. Since the real problem is not the size of the balance sheet but the size of reserves, this addresses the paper cut while ignoring the shark bite. The practical problem is that, after the Fed did "Operation Twist" in 2011—in which it exchanged short-term bonds in its portfolio for long-term bonds, in an effort to lower long-term rates—it only owned long-term bonds. Therefore, it would take more than a decade for the Fed to have the bonds simply mature. (Of these two problems, the theoretical problem is much bigger, but the practical problem is arguably more humorous since the Fed put itself in that position.)

Plan C: Conduct Massive and Long-Dated Reverse-Repurchase Operations

This is America. When something works, our natural reaction is to supersize it! So one possible solution was to take the normal mechanism for draining reserves and make it bigger. As I noted previously, the way the Fed's Open Market Desk effected policy in the pre-crisis days was to do *reverse repurchase* arrangements, in which the central bank lends the securities in its portfolio and takes in cash, which decreases the supply of reserves. Prior to the crisis, during the prior tightening phase, reverse repos subtracted as much as about $40 billion in reserves when the Fed wanted to tighten policy. So, the thinking goes, the mechanism works; all we have to do is increase it to about 60 times that size and the problem is solved.

The Fed began to test this arrangement in 2013. At the peak, about $600 billion in reverse repos were outstanding. About half of these were overnight repos, which are obviously of less interest since there is a practical limit to how many transactions you can roll over each and every day. The maximum amount of term reverses was $300 billion, and the terms (maturities) were on the order of one or two months. Still, that represents progress! Only another 10× and we could be there.

In mid-2014, however, interest in this solution waned somewhat as a pair of Fed officials expressed publicly the concern being felt among policymakers that there are significant limits to this strategy as well.[3] One of the concerns was that if the central bank sucks up a couple trillion in short-term money, then what happens to the other institutional structures (e.g., money funds) that would otherwise be the destination for this money? Especially, what happens in a crisis—would money funds collapse as investors moved their money to the Fed? Moreover, if the Fed is doing $40 billion in overnight repos, it has a ready set of counterparties in the primary dealer community. But if the Fed is doing $2.5 trillion, it needs a wider set of counterparties, and not all of them will necessarily be as creditworthy. These concerns were summarized in a paper published by the Divisions of Research and Statistics and Monetary Affairs at the Fed,[4] and the FOMC began looking for plan D.

Plan D: Just Move Interest Rates to Where We Want Them

The bankers are beginning to settle on the idea that interest rates can simply be manipulated by diktat, rather than through market operations, by changing the rates at which the Fed pays interest on reserves. An influential 2014 paper by Brian Sack and Joseph Gagnon suggested ways that the Fed could raise rates even without reducing the amount of excess reserves in the system.[5] Their approach would, indeed, succeed in moving interest rates. But the proposal, in the authors' own damning words, "appropriately [sic] ignores the quantity of money."

Considering that it is the quantity of money, not its price, that affects inflation—as hundreds of years of monetary history have proven beyond any reasonable doubt—this is a frightening view.

There is a crucial misunderstanding here, and it is unfortunately a fundamental tenet of the interest rate cult. Interest rates, when set in a free market system, are not the cause of money supply changes, but the result of them. The way the Fed operates tends to cause this confusion, because the Fed seems to adjust interest rates. But that is not, in fact, what happens. The Desk actually adjusts the level of reserves in the system, and reads the interest rate as an indication of whether reserves are at the right level (or at least, this was the way it was formerly done, before the "environment of abundant liquidity"). The confusion has gradually developed, and as I pointed out in Chapter 7, the institution has contributed to the confusion by gradually altering its policy statements to obfuscate what is actually going on. Let me repeat the key point again: Overnight interest rates are a measurement of the pressure on reserves.

Interest rates, in other words, are like a thermometer that measures the temperature in the body. The doctor plies his trade on a feverish patient with an eye on the thermometer. The doctor can't see the microbes and antibodies, but the thermometer tells him (her) if the treatment is working. In exactly the same way, the level of short-term interest rates tells the Fed if banks have in aggregate too many reserves or too few. But, continuing with the analogy, suppose the doctor lost sight of the real purpose of treatment? Suppose the doctor said, "Wow, this would be so much easier if I just put a little dial on the thermometer so that I could control the reading directly! Then I could just set it to the right temperature and I would be done." We would all recognize that doctor as a quack, and the patient would probably die.

As a side note, in the 1970s parents were told to plunge feverish kids into an icy bath to bring the body's temperature down. This is no longer the recommendation, as doctors recognize that controlling the temperature is not the same as controlling the cause of the temperature increase (and indeed, doing so is thought to short-circuit the body's natural signals and responses). So we continue to gradually retreat from the old practice of leeching a sick patient, except in monetary policy circles.

This approach, in effect, is what the Sack/Gagnon paper proposes. We want to control the temperature, so let's introduce a process that allows us to directly control the temperature! But this is wrong, because it is the reserve position that is critical to control; it is that which is out of control at the moment due to the presence of copious excess reserves, and the fact that the Fed can simply set the interest rate is irrelevant. Thought experiment: Why not have Congress set the legal interest rate at the "appropriate level" so that the Fed doesn't even need to do open market operations, ever? Hopefully, we can all see the absurdity in that.

The Sack/Gagnon plan, which as of now is the framework the Fed expects to use when it is time to tighten, will clearly permit the movement of interest rates to wherever the Fed wants them to be. But it will not solve the root problem, which is that the level of required reserves is essentially out of the Fed's control—which means the size of the money supply is out of its control as well, unless the adjustment of interest on excess reserves permits fine control of the reserves/money multiplier.

The plan misses the point a little bit anyway, because it isn't the rate that matters to monetary policy but the amount of transactional money (such as M2) in circulation. The Fed can set the overnight rate at 1 percent by simply agreeing to pay 1 percent as interest on excess reserves (IOER), which is essentially what the Sack/Gagnon paper proposes. But that won't do anything at all to M2, because it won't change the amount of reserves in the system and doesn't change the money multiplier that relates the quantity of those reserves to M2. Paying more interest on excess reserves would be a sweet present to banks, which would make more money by doing nothing, but it wouldn't change the size of reserve balances and hence would be unlikely to affect the money supply very much.

There is a mechanism by which the changing of interest paid on reserves may affect lending and hence the money supply, but it is important to understand that the underlying response is out of the Fed's hands and there is no way to calibrate it because the effect will vary. Here is how it works: If longer-term interest rates rise, but reserves have the same yield, then lending by banks becomes more profitable and loans will increase—that is, the money multiplier will rise, with less money in the vault and more money in transactional accounts. If, on the other hand, the Fed raises the interest on excess reserves while lending rates stay unchanged, then even fewer loans will be made and banks will hold more cash relative to loans. That is what the Fed hopes will happen: that they will raise overnight rates, but longer-term rates will not move much, so banks will lend less and M2 will decelerate. But it could easily work in the other direction, if the market pushes term rates higher, which spurs more lending; moreover, the general quality of available credits to lend to will also have an (unknown) effect since a certain amount of lending can have a different relative profitability, compared with reserves balances, depending on loan loss expectations.

In short, it is unlikely the Fed can meaningfully and pre-dictably change the growth rate of M2. It is essentially an exoge-nous variable now, for better or worse.

What about Velocity?

When we look at money supply growth, what seems fairly apparent is that its acceleration or deceleration is, more or less, out of the hands of central bankers operating in a regime of abundant liquidity. To put it bluntly, monetary policy's control of the money supply is dependent on adjustments made at the margin of required reserves, but that margin is buried under trillions of dollars' worth of excess liquidity—too much extra liquidity to quickly and painlessly drain. And, incidentally, this is not only true of policy in the United States: Though being earliest in the QE adventure, we are arguably the most far gone; other central banks are not dramatically behind. The ECB's balance sheet as I write this is currently some €2.5 trillion (about $2.3 trillion at current exchange rates), as Figure 9.2 illustrates. And the Bank of Japan sports a balance sheet—illustrated in Figure 9.3—of ¥350 trillion (about $2.8 trillion), too.

The other half of the controllable variables in the monetarist equation is money velocity. Figure 9.4 shows M2 velocity going back more than a half-century. A simple glance will tell you that velocity is incredibly low.

Money velocity is lower than in the 1960s, years before ATM machines and other financial innovations made it less important to be holding sums of cash for "precautionary" reasons, which lowered the equilibrium level of real cash balances at any interest rate and raised money velocity. It is lower than in the 1970s, when social upheavals and domestic policy uncertainty made investing for the long-term seem hopelessly optimistic and

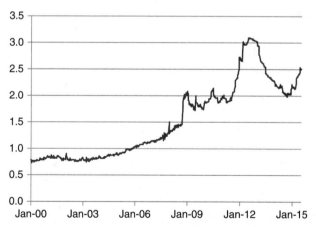

FIGURE 9.2 **Total assets of European Central Bank, trillions of euros**
Source: European Central Bank

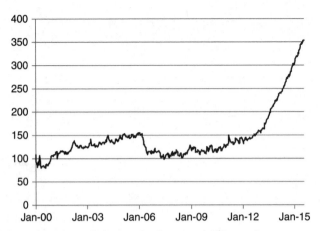

FIGURE 9.3 Total assets of the Bank of Japan, trillions of yen
Source: Bank of Japan

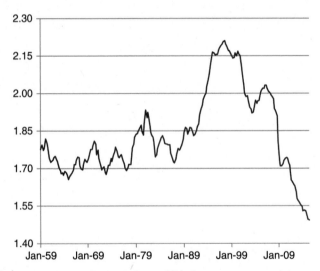

FIGURE 9.4 M2 money velocity is incredibly low.
Source: Federal Reserve Bank of St. Louis

living for now preferable, even necessary. And it is also lower than at the turn of the millennium with its low interest rates, high equities markets, and fear of the Y2K bug.

Money velocity mainly responds, as I pointed out in Chapter 3, to interest rates. But even if we also incorporate proxies for investor uncertainty, inflation expectations, and the attractiveness of other investments relative to cash, we cannot explain (with a linear model) why velocity is so low. Most likely, this means that the response of velocity to interest rates is nonlinear as rates get near zero. At some level, after broker and bank fees, taxes, and other transactions costs, the cost of holding an interest-bearing asset is greater than the potential benefit (at least in a risk-adjusted sense!), producing a negative expected yield for the investor. At that level, the demand for real cash balances might dramatically increase. It is only a hypothesis, but it is my best guess about what is happening.

Regardless of what is causing money velocity to be this low, it is plain that the bigger risk is a reversion to the long-term mean, probably because interest rates rise in a "normalization" of policy. The risk of such a reaction to normalization is large. In 2012, Samuel Reynard, an economist at the Swiss National Bank, published a paper[6] in which he incorporated the velocity response to higher interest rates into a model of money and inflation. A chart from that paper is shown in Figure 9.5 and illustrates how quantitative easing was likely to cause inflation in the future, especially since rising interest rates would increase money velocity along the way.

We are less concerned with timing in our current argument—"when" is less important than "whether," and the arguments in favor of a future rise in monetary velocity are compelling. For now, the key question is whether dramatic QE has any side effects we need to worry about and, if so, how large these side effects are and how they might manifest as policy is normalized. What is the range of feasible outcomes? Table 9.1 attempts one sort of answer. It is a what-if table that calculates the implications of the monetarist identity for a range of possible M2 money growth rates (on the vertical axis) and velocities (on the horizontal axis). In creating this table, I had to make a few assumptions, so I made them generously. Let us

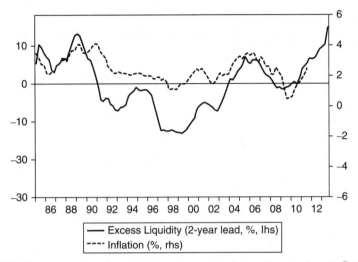

FIGURE 9.5 Integrating the velocity response to interest rates into inflation forecasts

Source: Peterson Institute for International Economics

TABLE 9.1 Inflation Outcomes Implied by Certain *M* and *V* Growth Rates

		Ending Velocity							
		1.4	1.5	1.6	1.7	1.8	1.9	2.0	2.1
M2 Growth Rate	2%	−3%	−1%	1%	3%	5%	7%	9%	11%
	3%	−2%	0%	2%	4%	6%	8%	10%	12%
	4%	−1%	1%	3%	5%	7%	9%	11%	13%
	5%	0%	2%	4%	6%	8%	10%	12%	14%
	6%	1%	3%	5%	7%	9%	11%	13%	15%
	7%	2%	4%	6%	8%	10%	12%	14%	16%
	8%	2%	5%	7%	9%	11%	13%	15%	17%

assume that somehow over the next three years, the United States achieves a 3 percent real growth rate. Then, for a given annualized growth in M2 and an ending velocity of *V*, what annualized inflation rate is implied over those 3 years? Put another way, for each entry in this table I calculated $MV \equiv PQ$

for a given M and V from the table and assuming a Q of 3 percent per year for 3 years, to find the change in P that is required for the equation to balance.

Note that a faster growth rate or a longer normalization period would lower the annualized inflation needed to balance the equation. But real growth much faster than 3 percent seems implausible and a normalization period much longer than three years seems to run counter to the expectations of investors and central bankers. However, if you don't like my figures, you can try out numbers you do like with the "MV Inflation Outcomes" calculator at http://www.enduringinvestments .com/calculators/.

I have highlighted two cells that may be of interest. The one in the left-hand part of the table is the result if money velocity does not change and money supply growth over the next three years slows to a 5 percent average. I think this is likely to be the best remotely likely outcome; in this case you get annualized inflation of about 2 percent, which is roughly where core inflation in the U.S. currently stands. That isn't bad at all, but note that it is above what is priced in (as of August 11, 2015) by inflation markets, which is about 1.25 percent for inflation over that period. Arguably, deflation is possible but it would require even lower money velocity and/or an inexplicable plunge in money supply growth—both of which seem to be remote possibilities at best.

The second highlighted cell shows the outcome if money supply growth hangs around 6 percent, but money velocity rises back to the level it was at the end of 2007 (which is also approximately the last time interest rates were "normal" at around 4 percent for five-year Treasuries). Note that this is more than the long-run average of M2 velocity, from Figure 9.4, of 1.85, but pretty close to the average level of 1980–2007. In such a case, which does not seem at all outlandish to me, you would see average price inflation of 13 percent per year. How's your money doing then? Even worse outcomes, of course, are possible and even feasible, as one moves to the lower right of the table.

What's wrong with money? This is what is wrong, today, with our money. Do not be fooled because we haven't yet impacted the pavement: The actions of many central bankers, led by the Federal Reserve, have exposed our money to an almost assured, significant loss in purchasing power over the next several years. Whether that turns into something worse is as unknowable as the precise length at which a stretched rubber band will snap.

How much time do we have before these things begin to happen? I would answer that until interest rates begin to normalize, we have probably not yet confronted the moment of truth when lazy central banking comes back to haunt us.

After the rate normalization campaign begins, it is also not clear how long it will take before the wheels come off and velocity rises, or money growth surges, or inflation leaps. This is not a cop-out; it is a fundamental quality of critical points in complex systems that we can't know exactly when the break happens.

If a length of steel is flexed, it is impossible to know *exactly* when it will fail. We can, however, figure out when that critical point is approaching, and estimate the probabilities of structural failure for a given load. These are just probabilities, and of course such an estimate depends on our knowledge of the structural properties of the piece of steel.

With economies and financial markets, the science has not yet advanced enough for us to say that we know the "structural properties" of economies and markets. And yet, we can measure the stress markets are under by measuring departures from normalcy and make observations about the degree of risk.

Didier Sornette wrote a book in 2003 called *Why Stock Markets Crash: Critical Events in Complex Financial Systems*.[7] It is a terrific read for anyone interested in studying these questions and exploring the developing science of critical points in financial markets. His work goes a long way toward explaining why it is so easy to identify a bubble and yet so hard to predict the timing of its demise.

So in that spirit, let us look at a few pictures that illuminate the degree of "departures from normalcy" which economies and markets currently manifest. Figure 9.6 shows the nice relationship between the increase in GDP-adjusted money supply (M/Q from Figure 3.1) and the increase in the price level (P) over the nice, regular period between 1962 and 1992. I've added to this plot a dot representing the latest 10-year period, and (for fun) a dot representing the 10 years ending in the heat of the stock market bubble in 1999. Do we appear to be out of normalcy?

Figure 9.7 shows the relationship between stocks and spot commodity prices, as represented by the S&P 500 and the Bloomberg Commodity Index. The two sets of points represent the periods from 1991 to 1997 (black triangles) and 2003 to

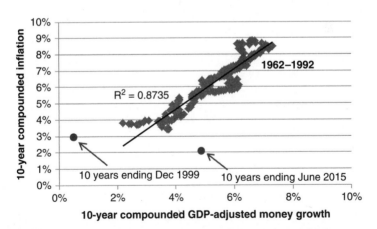

FIGURE 9.6 Compounded money growth versus compounded inflation, 10-year periods

Source: Bureau of Economic Analysis, Federal Reserve, Bureau of Labor Statistics

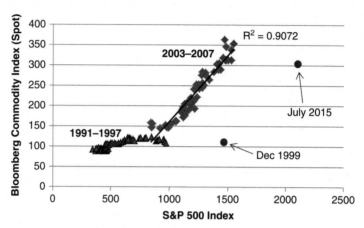

FIGURE 9.7 **Stocks versus spot commodity prices**
Source: Bloomberg Indices, Standard & Poor's

2007 (blue diamonds); in other words, 1991 to 2007, excluding
the period around the equity bubble (1998–2002). I have drawn
a regression on the 2003 to 2007 segment, which has a strong—
and sensible—fit. Applying that fit to the 1991–1997 period, it
suggests that in the early part of the 1990s, stock prices were
probably too low or commodities prices too high. This makes
intuitive sense to me in a period when stocks were out of favor
in an environment still prone to worry a lot about inflation. As
the 1990s developed, though, concern about inflation ebbed,
and commodities languished while stocks soared. The two
isolated red dots show the current point and the point from
December 1999. The question again is: Do we appear out
of normalcy?

Let's try one more. Figure 9.8 shows the same commodity
index, but this time against the money supply (divided by GDP).
It makes sense that spot commodities over time should move
more or less in relation to the aggregate amount of money in
circulation. The relative prices of two items are at least somewhat related to their relative scarcities. We will trade a lot of
sand for one diamond, because there's a lot of sand and very

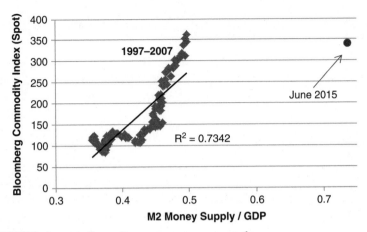

FIGURE 9.8 **Commodity prices versus money supply**
Source: Federal Reserve, Bloomberg Indices

few diamonds. But if diamonds suddenly rained down from the sky for some reason, the price of diamonds relative to sand would plummet. We would see this as a decline in the dollar price of diamonds relative to the dollar price of sand, which would presumably be stable, but the dollar in such a case plays only the role of a "unit of account" to compare these two assets. The price of diamonds falls, in dollars, because there are lots more diamonds and no change in the amount of dollars. But if the positions were reversed and there were lots more dollars, then the price of dollars should fall relative to the price of diamonds. In this case, dollars have been raining from the sky and yet their price relative to commodities has not fallen—that is, the nominal price of commodities has not risen, as we would have expected. Figure 9.8 shows that the price of money, relative to hard assets like physical commodities, may be in the greatest bubble it has ever been in. And since, unlike stocks and unlike real estate, everybody holds money, this may be the biggest bubble of them all.

All three of these figures—and I could have chosen many others—show a highly flexed economy and highly flexed markets. A break in this steel bar is almost assured; the only question is when.

Moreover, while we hear so much today about the "coming deflationary depression," I have to say that with the quantity of reserves in the system and the direction in which the monetary pictures are flexed, there is in my opinion as much chance of a deflationary outcome as I have of being appointed prime minister of Egypt.

I should also point out that I am not super concerned about the "depression" part of the phrase. Clearly, the massive expansion of aggregate reserves has not had an important effect on real economic growth over the last half-decade. Therefore, it strikes me as likely that the unwind will also not have a dramatic effect on real growth. I don't expect widespread bank failures in this next crack-up, and unemployment may not approach the highs from the financial crisis but show a more normal cyclical swing in the next recession. Still, higher inflation adds friction to the economic system, and lowers the long-term growth rate we can expect. This is why Fed Chairmen used to remark that the Fed could best achieve maximum long-term growth by ensuring that inflation stayed low and stable. Interestingly, we no longer hear that remark.

When (not if) the break to higher inflation happens, the consequence for our money, and hence the lifestyles of the unprotected, will be severe. This is because inflation has "long tails." That is, when inflation happens, it tends to keep happening. Over the last 100 years, inflation in the United States has most frequently been between 2 percent and 4 percent per annum. However, inflation has been over 4 percent fully 31 percent of the time during that century. More importantly, the probability that inflation was over 10 percent, given that it was over 4 percent, was 32 percent. In other words, once inflation exceeds 4 percent, historically about one-third of the time it will be above 10 percent! That is what we mean by "long

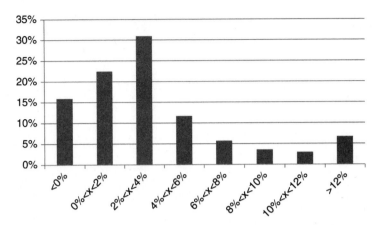

FIGURE 9.9 **Frequency of year-over-year inflation rates, 1915–2015**
Source: Bureau of Labor Statistics, author's calculations

tails." Figure 9.9 shows this graphically. You can see that the distribution is anything but a normal distribution. Inflation is either low, or it isn't. And if it isn't, it may well be quite high.

Moreover, inflation tends to go from low to high fairly quickly. Figure 9.10 shows the historical record in a manner that will surprise readers who were raised mainly in the period of declining inflation over the last 30 years. It shows that the percentage of time over the last 100 years that inflation accelerated by "at least X percent" from one year to the next, where X is shown on the x-axis.

So, not surprisingly, inflation accelerated about half the time (the first point in Figure 9.10 shows that 50 percent of the time, inflation accelerated "at least 0 percent.") Inflation accelerated at least 1 percent year over year in about 32 percent of the periods. Look at the long tails! When inflation was rising, one-fifth of the time it rose at least 2 percent over one year; one-tenth of the time it rose at least 4 percent! Thus, if inflation is currently 2 percent, statistically we would say there is a 1-in-10 chance that next year it will be above 6 percent. Does that seem shocking? If so, that is because you are recalling several

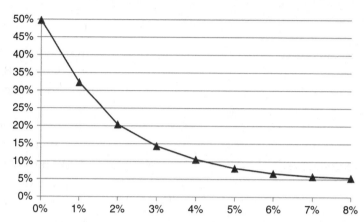

FIGURE 9.10 **Frequency of acceleration of at least** *X* **percent in inflation compared to one year ago, 1915–2015**
Source: Bureau of Labor Statistics, author's calculations

decades of secular inflation decline. Actually, if we exclude from Figure 9.10 the times that inflation rose over the last 30 years of secular disinflation, the picture is even worse.

Is it fair to exclude the last 30 years in that way? Perhaps not in a strict quantitative sense, since if you exclude all of the boring periods all you have left are exciting periods. But I would argue that Figures 9.6, 9.7, and 9.8 suggest that another 30 years of relative calm on the inflation front (and certainly another 30 years of disinflation) is a long-odds bet. If that is true, then the volatile 1970s might be a better analog for the future than the go-go 1990s.

In conclusion, what's wrong with money? Our money is like a 1975 Ford Pinto that is still on the road today. The good news is that it has survived this long, and may well make it another few miles. The bad news is that it also might explode at any moment. We are defying the odds. Is there anything we can do to decrease the chances of disaster?

Notes

1. Janet L. Yellen, "The Federal Reserve's Asset Purchase Program," Allied Social Science Associations Annual Meeting, January 8, 2011. Available at http://www.federalreserve.gov/newsevents/speech/yellen20110108a.htm.
2. Brian P. Sack, "Preparing for a Smooth (Eventual) Exit," Remarks at the National Association for Business Economics Policy Conference, Arlington, Virginia, March 8, 2010. Link: http://www.newyorkfed.org/newsevents/speeches/2010/sac100308.html.
3. "Two Fed Officials Suggest Reverse Repos May Need Borrowing Limits, After All," by Michael S. Derby on *The Wall Street Journal*'s Real Time Economics blog. Link: http://blogs.wsj.com/economics/2014/06/11/two-fed-officials-suggest-reverse-repos-may-need-borrowing-limits-after-all/.
4. Josh Frost, Lorie Logan, Antoine Martin, Patrick McCabe, Fabio Natalucci, and Julie Remache (2015). "Overnight RRP Operations as a Monetary Policy Tool: Some Design Considerations," Finance and Economics Discussion Series 2015-010. Washington: Board of Governors of the Federal Reserve System, http://dx.doi.org/10.17016/FEDS.2015.010.
5. Brian Sack and Joseph Gagnon, "Monetary Policy with Abundant Liquidity: A New Operating Framework for the Federal Reserve," Peterson Institute for International Economics, January 2014. Available at http://www.iie.com/publications/interstitial.cfm?ResearchID=2558.
6. Samuel Reynard, "Assessing Potential Inflation Consequences of QE after Financial Crises," Working Paper Series WP 12-22, Peterson Institute for International Economics, November 2012.
7. Didier Sornette, *Why Stock Markets Crash: Critical Events in Complex Financial Systems* (Princeton, NJ: Princeton University Press, 2003).

CHAPTER 10

My Prescription

I have spent many pages arguing for how extremely messed up our current predicament is. I have detailed a series of proposals that policymakers have explored to defuse the monetary pipe-bomb that could blow at any moment, and argued that none of those proposals will work. So how is it that I have a proposal that I believe has a chance of working?

Let's not kid ourselves. The time for easy solutions is long gone. If we could roll back the clock, the easiest solution was to eschew quantitative easing altogether. It was ineffective if the purpose was to accelerate growth, and it was poorly designed (encouraging reserves formation, rather than money formation) if its purpose was to prevent deflation (or to encourage growth under an erroneous interpretation of monetary causality). If we give central banks a pass on QE1 because times were scary, then the next-best solution would have been to start unwinding the extraordinary policy once the extraordinary times had passed—certainly, no later than 2010, when economies were growing and banks were no longer failing, and inflation outside of the housing sector was not threatening anything like deflation.

But those opportunities were missed.

Central bankers, at least in the United States, now give lip service to the need to "normalize" policy. Unfortunately, they are on the verge of doing this in the absolutely worst way possible, failing to address the huge quantity of excess reserves while encouraging money velocity to rise by hiking rates by declaration.

Stop!

If we go back to the original problem, we can see the glimmer of a solution. The main problem is that if money velocity rises, most likely because interest rates are rising, then inflation will rise unless money growth can be reined in. However, money growth cannot be reined in because there are too many "excess" reserves in the system. This means that money growth is not under the control of a central bank whose tools operate at the margin of required reserves.

There are two focal points of monetarism we need to control. The quantity of transactional money balances (M2), and the velocity of those balances (V). Currently, we have no control over M2, and the only control we can exercise on V is to cause its increase. Therefore, it is of signal importance that we regain control over the margin; it is crucial that we restore to the Federal Reserve the ability to slow money growth by restricting required reserves.

The solution is highly unconventional, but has a chance of working (in contrast to the solution currently being considered).

First, the Federal Reserve should change the reserve requirement for banks. If the mountain will not come to Mohammed, then Mohammed must go to the mountain. In this case, the Fed has the power (and the authority) to, at a stroke, redefine reserves so that all of the current "excess" reserves essentially become "required" reserves, by changing the amount of reserves banks are required to hold against loans. No longer would there be a risk of banks cracking open the "boxes of currency" in their vaults to extend more loans and create more money than is healthy for an economy that seeks noninflationary growth. There would be no chance of a reversion to the mean of the money multiplier, which would be devastating to the inflation picture. And the Open Markets Desk at the Fed would immediately regain power over short-term interest rates, because when they add or subtract reserves in open market operations, banks would care.

To be sure, this would be awful news for the banks themselves and their stock prices would likely take a hit. It would amount to a forcible deleveraging, and impair potential profitability as a result. But we should recognize that such a deleveraging has already happened, and this policy would merely recognize *de jure* what has already happened *de facto*.

Movements in reserve requirements have historically been very rare, and this is probably why such a solution is not being considered as far as I know. The reserve requirement is considered a "blunt instrument," and you can imagine how a movement in the requirement could under normal circumstances lead to extreme volatility as the quantity of required reserves suddenly lurched from approximate balance into significant surplus or deficit. But that is not our current problem. Our current problem cries out for a blunt instrument!

While the Fed is making this adjustment, and as it prepares to press money growth lower, they should work to keep medium-term interest rates low, not raise them, so that money velocity does not abruptly normalize. Interest rates should be normalized slowly, letting velocity rise gradually while money growth is pushed lower simultaneously. This would cause the yield curve to flatten substantially as tighter monetary conditions cause short-term interest rates in the United States to rise.

Of course, in time the Fed should relinquish control of term rates altogether, and should also allow its balance sheet to shrink naturally. It is possible that, as this happens, reserve requirements could be edged incrementally back to normal as well. But those decisions are years away.

I doubt that this course of action could be enacted without dislocations, perhaps significant, of economy and markets. But as my high school economics teacher, Bill Childs, told us many years ago: In economics, there are never any solutions—only trade-offs.

It is time for smarter trade-offs.

How to Invest with Inflation in Mind

In Part III, we take the important step of implementation. How might you actually arrange your investments to prepare for the various possible scenarios (many of which are quite ugly)? The implications of Table 9.1 in Part II are important and extremely relevant for the investment process. Higher inflation rates will tend to be accompanied by higher interest rates. Higher interest rates, of course, imply lower bond prices; as bond prices fall, then the equilibrium prices of other asset classes which compete with bonds (such as, but not limited to, equities) will also be likely to fall. So Table 9.1 contains a warning not just for the cost of living, but for asset allocation decisions as well. Note that there is no *prediction* associated with that table. It is merely a statement of *possibilities*, of reasonably plausible potential outcomes.

You may put different weights on the probabilities of those potential outcomes than I do. But regardless of what your probability matrix looks like, there is no denying that inflation is a *risk factor*. It is a risk factor that is critically important in finance theory, which tends to speak of the investment problem as "maximizing the inflation-adjusted after-tax return over time." Investors can improve on that definition, as I will show later.

Building an inflation-aware portfolio isn't difficult, and doesn't have to mean a wildly exotic approach. But most investors—and many investment advisers—treat inflation as such a low-probability event that there is no reason to consider it in portfolio construction. Approaches I have seen, from major brokerage houses in fact, will nod to inflation by incorporating an "inflation assumption" that is used to adjust Social Security cash flows, for example—but that is *fixed* at, say, 2 percent. That's not inflation-aware; it is inflation-obtuse.

Unfortunately, the answer for how you should build an inflation-aware portfolio isn't as simple as "buy fewer bonds and more commodities," or Part III could be much shorter than it is!

Most investors focus on the investment portfolio as a stand-alone entity. This is natural since theorists have until relatively recently focused on the trade-off between a portfolio's risk and return. It was assumed that there was a single "optimal" portfolio that best balanced risk and return or, at best, a single curve of optimal portfolios the choice among which depended on the investor's risk/return trade-off preference. This is why many brokers have a "model portfolio" that tracks the analysts' recommendations, along with the recommendations of the asset allocation committee.

But the model portfolio doesn't make any sense for many investors. Nor can most "rules of thumb," such as the old saw that an investor should have an equity allocation equal to 120 minus his age, be universal. Aside from the obvious absurdity that it implies a 16-year-old should have a leveraged equity portfolio, with a higher-than-100 percent allocation, it would be weird indeed if by some bizarre coincidence of modern finance it just happened that the optimal allocation turned out to be linear in time. It would be like discovering that the number of people in any given room of a particular age was always 70 minus the age. Why would we expect such symmetry between unrelated quantities? Moreover, it is curious that not all authorities agree what number we should subtract our age from. It seems that more equity-minded shops recommend a higher number. I am not sure why that should be. Finally, I don't know how that rule changes when I add asset classes. If I am considering only stocks and bonds, and the formula is 120 minus my age, then is that still the right allocation to equities if I can invest in stocks, bonds, real estate, hedge funds, commodities, and inflation-linked bonds? I am pretty sure the answer is no.

Figuring out the "right" portfolio for you is *not* simple, and if you are looking for simple answers you have come to the wrong place. On the other hand, if you keep reading from here, it implies you are willing to put some work into the question. The good news is that the fundamental truths about organizing your financial life are, at the end of the day, fairly simple. It is the application of those truths to your own personal situation that calls for deep introspection.

Occasionally, I will be asked for some investment advice in a taxi, or in an elevator, or in some other place where a lengthy exposition is not possible. In these circumstances I have distilled everything down to "the three miracles of finance":

1. Thrift
2. Compound interest
3. Rebalancing

Some people think that all you have to do in order to make money in the long run is to own equities, because "stocks always rise in the long run." This is wrong, or at least is right only in the most useless of ways: If you own stocks for 40 or 50 years, then you're reasonably likely to outperform inflation by a little bit—as long as you don't panic when the market plunges, you reinvest your dividends, and you are not so unlucky as to invest when valuations are high and sell when valuations are low. But that isn't a fundamental truth. There is no mathematical reason that stocks must always rise in the long run, and there are many cases that can be pointed to as examples of periods where stocks lost ground to inflation over a very long period of time. However, each of the three "miracles" I've listed above are mathematical certainties,[1] and we will begin this part by talking about them in more detail.

Note

1. It is possible to contrive examples where *rebalancing* isn't guaranteed to work, but those examples require characteristics of markets that, if they were real, would make it much easier to trade markets and to make money. That is, markets would have to have low amounts of "noise" in them, extremely low levels of volatility, or both. We do not observe markets like this in real life.

CHAPTER 11

Only Three Miracles

A nyone who pitches you a solution without a cost, or a risk, should be suspected immediately. Although markets are not efficient—certainly not in the strict academic sense, and probably not in the practical sense of it being difficult for even skilled practitioners to add consistent value—markets most of the time do not offer free lunches. If you want greater return, you generally must take additional risk.

For example, suppose you don't like the 3 percent yield on long-term Treasuries, so you buy a corporate bond yielding 5 percent. Here is the test question: What is your expected return?

Unless there is something systematically wrong with the market—and as I said, *sometimes* there is, as when credit spreads were woefully mispriced in early 2009—then your expected return is about 3 percent: 5 percent in interest, minus 2 percent in expected credit losses over time for a portfolio of similar bonds. If you actually earn 5 percent, it means you got a lucky draw instead of the −50 percent in a default. If you play the game over and over, you will expect to make +5, +5, +5, +5, +5, −50, +5, with the minus-50s dragging just enough from your portfolio to bring your average return to 3 percent (if, again, the market is fairly priced). But you cannot treat that 5 percent as the expected return; optimization routines that use current yields for corporate bonds as the expected return are simply wrong.

So there are no miracles in asset pricing. You can't get rich in the short term by asset allocation, unless you also have luck. But there are three miracles that are *guaranteed* to make your future life better, and which do not depend on luck.

Thrift

The first of these is *thrift*. I know that this sounds incredibly pedestrian and boring, but good investing is in fact pedestrian and boring (Jack Bogle figured out an investing age ago that the *really, really* boring issue of economizing on management fees can add substantially to your long-term return). I want to share a profound observation my father once shared with me. He told me that the difference between living slightly *within* your means and living slightly *beyond* your means, in the near-term, isn't very much. If your income is $5,000 per month, then the difference between spending $4,900 per month and spending $5,100 per month isn't very much. But the difference in the *long run* from that modest expression of thrift is truly profound. In Figure 11.1, I show the savings of two hypothetical

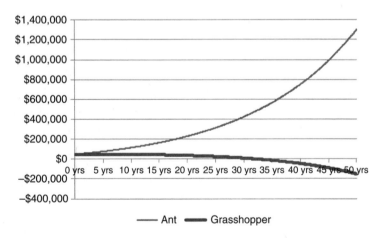

FIGURE 11.1 **The ant and the grasshopper**

individuals over time. They both start with $50,000 in savings; individual A (the "ant") saves $200 per month from his income, increasing that amount every month with a 2 percent inflation rate, while individual B (the "grasshopper") spends $200 per month over and above his income, increasing his withdrawals by inflation every month to keep the real amount stable. I assume a real, compounded return of 3 percent per year on both portfolios. The figure shows what happens to their portfolio values over time. Note that the difference in consumption between the ant's lifestyle and the grasshopper's lifestyle was a mere $400 per month; but the difference in long-term outcomes puts one in the penthouse and the other in the outhouse.

To put it in a slightly pithier way: If your income is less than your outgo, then your upkeep is your downfall.

That is Miracle 1: A penny saved is a penny earned, and those pennies matters a great deal over time.

Compound Interest

Actually, a penny saved is not a penny earned, but a penny compounded. And here is the second miracle of modern finance, which you don't have to do anything special to achieve: compound interest. This isn't exactly cutting-edge finance, but I find the miracle of compounding is really underappreciated. If people generally realized how important compounding is, no one would be fooled by the charlatan who claims "true" inflation has been 8.5 percent over the last 40 years, rather than 2.5 percent (see Chapter 6). It is such an *obviously* absurd statement—but only if you have some appreciation of the awesome power of compounding over long periods.

Compounding, of course, merely means "interest on interest." If you earn 5 percent on your investment of $100, then in year 2 you have $105. But in year 3, you have $100, plus the $5 of interest you earned in year 1, plus $5 more interest you earned in year 2 on the original $100, plus $0.25 of interest you earned on the first year's interest. In the next year, you earn another $5 on the original $100, plus $0.26 on the first $5 of interest and the $0.25 it earned last year, plus $0.25 on the second $5 payment, plus another $5. Figure 11.2 shows how this evolves over time. The bottom rectangular area is your original principal. The middle wedge represents how much additional money you have just from the simple interest ($5 per year in this case). The top line shows the accumulation of interest on interest (on interest on interest . . .). After 60 years, your account now has $1,867.92, of which $100 (which is now only 5 percent of the total) is your original investment, $300 (16 percent) is your simple interest, and $1,467.92 (79 percent) is your interest on interest.

You have almost certainly heard of this miracle, but maybe you haven't appreciated the implications, of which I will mention but four:

1. You don't have to look for compounding. It finds you. It is a mathematical fact. It costs nothing.
2. Investing early is more important than what you invest in, over long periods. If you invest a lump sum for 30 years

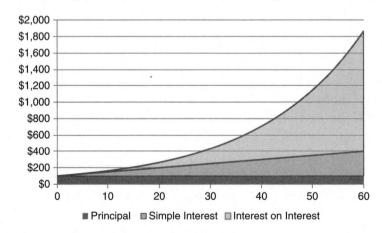

FIGURE 11.2 **The power of interest on interest**

at 4 percent, you are ahead of the guy who invested the same lump sum for 20 years at 6 percent. And if you combine this with the thrift observation, the person who invests $100 per month for 30 years at 4 percent crushes (by almost 20 percent!) the guy who invests $100 per month for only 20 years but earned 8 percent.

3. The miracle of compound interest doesn't work if you don't give the market anything to compound. If you take distributions of your interest or dividends, you lose the top line in Figure 11.2. Your account has the bottom line as the balance all of the time; you have spent the middle line; and the top line is just *gone*.

4. Compound interest may be more valuable than compounded uncertain returns. This is less obvious than the prior three points, but it follows because the nature of compounding works both ways. Negative returns are worse in series than alone. Consider the following example of three investments that each has a simple expected return of 6 percent per year, or 0.5 percent per month. The first investment has no variance; that is, each month it pays 0.5 percent on the balance, which compounds over time. The second one has a 2 percent monthly standard deviation; that is, each month the *expected* return is 0.5 percent, and with a two-thirds probability it may be between −1.5 percent and +2.5 percent (and one-third of the time it will be outside that range). The third investment has a 4 percent monthly standard deviation, so it also has an expectation of 0.5 percent monthly returns but the two-thirds range is −3.5 percent to +4.5 percent. (This is not quite as volatile as the stock market. The S&P 500's standard deviation has averaged a bit higher than 4.25 percent per month since 1990).

I subjected this scenario to a Monte Carlo simulation of 1,000 trials for each investment.[1] Figure 11.3 shows the median total

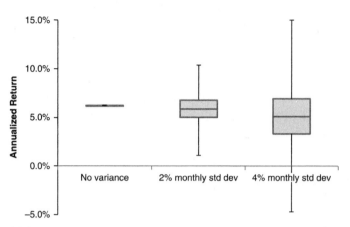

FIGURE 11.3 **Compounding interest may be better than compounding uncertain returns.**

return for 30 years, plus the high, third quartile, first quartile, and low of the range of outcomes.

The salient point here isn't the width of the ranges, but that the median return (where half of the returns were better, and half were worse) was lower the higher that volatility got. An important point is worth mentioning here: The average return, as opposed to the median return, is actually higher in the more volatile cases. This happens because long upward tails outweigh long downward tails that are bounded by zero. Exactly the same thing happens if you look at average payouts at the slot machines in a casino. Because a couple of people hit big jackpots, the average return to playing slots doesn't look that bad. But more relevant to the player who goes in and pulls the lever once or twice is the median return, in which half of the gambling sessions will be better and half of them will be worse. Most of us will not hit the jackpot!

Volatility is "bad" for several reasons, but not least of which is that it has negative effects on your median outcome because of the power of compounding. Again, this causes problems with certain illustrations you see from some investment advisers.

Of course a 3 percent return is better than a 1 percent return if they are both equally variable, but if the investment producing the 3 percent return is much more variable, then it isn't as clear which is the winner. But many arguments about stocks "for the long run" suggest that simply because the expectation for equities is better over long periods of time, they're naturally better over much shorter periods of time that can still seem quite long to a normal investor—like, say, five years. This is not as clear as they make it sound, even if it can be shown that equities at times have very good expected long-run returns.

So the message from this second miracle is this: Do not underappreciate the value of steady gains. And do not underestimate the value of reinvesting interest and dividends.

Rebalancing

Volatility, though, isn't all bad. How would you buy low and sell high if there were no lows and highs?

The reason that rebalancing adds returns is that rebalancing to neutral weights is a systematic method by which you are selling what goes up, because you now have too much of it, and buying what goes down, because you now don't have enough of it. That's one way to buy low and sell high! In order to have significant returns to a rebalancing strategy, however, several things need to be true: The assets need to have reasonably high volatility as well as a low correlation between them. If all of the assets are moving together, there is obviously no important benefit from switching between them.

Here is an experiment that illustrates how rebalancing can affect one's returns. Figure 11.4 shows a total return index for two strategies involving a portfolio of four assets: crude oil, copper, coffee, and sugar. This is obviously a fairly diverse group of commodities. One strategy delivers just the price return from the front futures contract (I didn't adjust for the

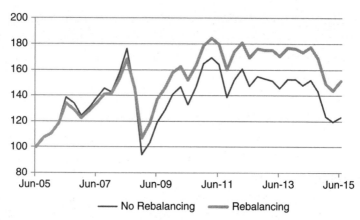

FIGURE 11.4 **Quarterly rebalancing of crude, copper, coffee, and sugar portfolio**

rolls; the absolute return isn't important, only the relative return of one strategy versus the other), assuming an initial investment of 25 percent in each asset and no rebalancing. That produces the thin, red line. If the portfolio is rebalanced quarterly, then we get the result shown in blue. Rebalancing produced a return of about 2.2 percent per year in this case.

By contrast, Figure 11.5 shows an analogous experiment with four equity indices: the MSCI EAFE Index, the S&P 500

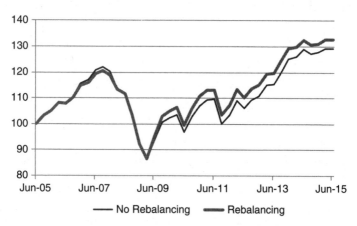

FIGURE 11.5 **Quarterly rebalancing of portfolio of four equity indices**

Index, the Russell 2000 Value Index, and the Russell 2000 Growth Index. The rebalancing return here is worth a mere 0.27 percent per year. As I said, there is not much benefit to rebalancing between things that are moving in unison. It doesn't matter how often you change lanes, if all of the lanes are moving at the same speed!

Now, if you have a portfolio of *individual* equities, rather than indices, then you have a better chance of realizing some rebalancing return. However, even in that case it is important to realize that most of an equity's return is a market return: That is, in a bull market almost all stocks rise and in a bear market almost all stocks fall.

But when we look at your overall portfolio in terms of asset-class balance, rather than securities, we can see that the correlations between different asset classes such as stocks, bonds, commodities, and so on are not as high as the correlations between individual stocks. Thus, the value of rebalancing from time to time away from well-performing asset classes and into poorly performing asset classes can be quite large.

Note

1. In a Monte Carlo simulation one generates random paths subject to certain rules—in this case, that monthly returns are pulled randomly from a normal distribution of $\mu = 0.5\%$, $\rho = 0\%$, 2%, or 4%, depending on the scenario.

CHAPTER 12

Inflation-Aware Investing and the Easy Way[1]

The problem with writing about investment approaches is that every person's investing problem is different and, therefore, requires different treatment. Moreover, the more "sophisticated" approaches require some experience to implement. Monte Carlo simulations don't merely fall out of the box, ready to go; they must be loaded with good data and return estimates, and developing these is not trivial. Even highly esteemed brokerage shops don't always give good input data, even when they have elaborate tools (a popular assumption, for example, is that future returns are accurately described by historical returns, which is not only a bad assumption but is guaranteed to be the most wrong when assets are mispriced in a bubble—with the best expected returns happening when historical returns are calculated to the current high prices, implying that you should have heavy investments when prices are already high: exactly the wrong thing to do). My first caution, then, is that sophistication is not the same as, or a substitute for, experience. And this is truer the more complex your financial situation is.

Incidentally, one way that financial advisers absolutely earn their pay is to help you manage taxes. In this chapter, I abstract from the tax question but a good financial adviser can help you optimize your plan by choosing which investments to make in,

143

say, tax-advantaged or tax-exempt accounts rather than taxable accounts. There is no tax advice in this chapter.

Nor, for legal reasons (since I run an investment management firm), is there any investment advice *per se*. What my goal is in this chapter is to give you some general guidance and introduce more useful rules of thumb, along with some handy little charts to keep around.

It makes sense here to repeat an admonition from earlier in this book, advanced under a different context: I try hard to help you ask the right questions, rather than to give you the right answers. Now in investment management, more so than in economic forecasting, we can strive to be "right" with a better chance of success but the same basic philosophy applies.

As an aside, also note what "success" means in the financial planning context. Your plan is the "right" plan if it gave you the best *a priori* expected result for the given level of risk you were willing to take. The actual after-the-fact result and risk delivered by the market is an unfair way to evaluate a financial advisor. If the adviser, in consultation with you, decided on an investment approach that could potentially lose 30 percent, and then it actually lost 30 percent because the market bombed, then that is not necessarily a failure. But if that same investment instead lost 50 percent, or if you had told the advisor that you can't lose more than 10 percent and the adviser caused you to be invested in ways that lost 30 percent, then it is a failure. Moreover, it may also be a failure if you told the adviser that you don't like to take much risk, and the investments he or she encouraged you to make actually *gained* 70 percent. Nice result, but not the "right" plan for someone who doesn't like volatility.

We focus here on looking at the problem in the right way, and making some generalizations that will push you toward smarter portfolio decisions. To avoid a one-size-fits-all prescription for investing in an inflation-aware way, I will discuss one broad approach here and a more-involved approach in Chapter 13.

The Easy Way

Investing the "easy way" doesn't necessarily mean that it is a bad way. Sophistication isn't the same as accuracy, or usefulness, either! A super-sophisticated approach that you won't use or don't understand is not very helpful. So the "easy way" is designed merely to get you on the road to "inflation-aware" investing.

The three miracles of thrift, compounding, and rebalancing are important components to any plan. General thrift is up to you, but thrift in an investment context means paying extra investment fees only if you receive extra benefits. When you want equity market exposure, direct equity investing or buying index funds are the thriftiest approaches. This doesn't mean you should not ever pay for active management, merely that if you pay for an active bond or stock manager you should be sure they are adding more than enough value, consistently, to cover the added costs and the risks associated with deviating from passive weights.

With respect to compounding, remember to reinvest interest and dividends whenever you can. As for rebalancing, revisit and rebalance your plan at least annually, or any time market moves cause your portfolio weights to move more than some threshold amount (I like 5 percent, but it is up to you. Higher percentages mean less rebalancing, lower costs from rebalancing, and a bigger impact when you do rebalance, but more missed opportunities for smaller rebalances).

For the simple approach, we are going to lean on a few straightforward tables showing three major asset classes: stocks, bonds, and inflation-indexed bonds. Table 12.1 is similar to a table shown in a relatively famous study on retirement, known as the Trinity Study.[2] That paper, published in 1998, used historical sampling methods to determine the range of outcomes that historically would have resulted from a particular combination of asset allocation and withdrawal policies.[3] For example,

TABLE 12.1   **Inflation-Adjusted Portfolio Success Rates, Monte Carlo Simulation**

	Withdrawal Rate as a % of Initial Portfolio Value									
Payout Period	3%	4%	5%	6%	7%	8%	9%	10%	11%	12%
100% Stocks										
15 Years	99	96	88	77	64	50	37	25	17	11
20 Years	96	87	71	58	42	30	20	14	8	5
25 Years	90	78	60	43	29	19	13	6	4	2
30 Years	83	68	48	34	23	14	9	6	2	1
35 Years	78	59	42	28	18	10	6	4	2	1
75% Stocks/25% Bonds										
15 Years	100	99	94	84	68	49	33	17	12	6
20 Years	98	93	79	59	41	23	13	6	3	1
25 Years	95	83	62	43	24	11	6	3	1	1
30 Years	92	72	49	28	16	8	3	1	1	0
35 Years	84	62	39	24	12	5	3	1	0	0
50% Stocks/50% Bonds										
15 Years	100	100	98	89	70	45	24	12	4	2
20 Years	100	96	84	58	34	15	6	2	0	0
25 Years	99	88	63	33	14	5	2	0	0	0
30 Years	96	75	44	21	7	2	0	0	0	0
35 Years	89	59	33	14	5	2	1	0	0	0
25% Stocks/75% Bonds										
15 Years	100	100	99	92	67	35	14	5	1	0
20 Years	100	98	85	53	22	6	1	0	0	0
25 Years	99	89	57	23	6	1	0	0	0	0
30 Years	97	74	34	10	2	0	0	0	0	0
35 Years	89	56	22	6	1	0	0	0	0	0
100% Bonds										
15 Years	100	100	97	85	56	28	10	3	1	0
20 Years	100	96	75	38	15	5	1	0	0	0
25 Years	97	79	43	15	3	1	0	0	0	0
30 Years	91	58	22	6	1	0	0	0	0	0
35 Years	80	39	12	2	0	0	0	0	0	0

Note: Numbers rounded to the nearest whole percentage
Source: Michael Ashton, "Managing Laurels: Liability-Driven Investment for Professional Athletes," Table 4.

Cooley et al. established that given a portfolio mix of 75 percent stocks and 25 percent bonds and a withdrawal rate of 6 percent of the initial portfolio value, for a 30-year holding period (over the historical interval covered by the study), the portfolio would have failed 32 percent of the time for, conversely, a 68 percent success rate. In a paper I wrote in 2011 for the Society of Actuaries monograph on retirement security[4] and extended in a paper addressing the problems of the professional athlete retiree,[5] I updated and extended the analysis of the Trinity Study using a Monte Carlo simulation that allows for more flexible assumptions and modeling. For example, we can replace the historical return record with one based on whatever mean returns and variances we like, and whatever covariance matrix we believe represents reality. More importantly, we can extend such analysis to other asset classes that were not studied in the Trinity Study. And still *more* important is that we can examine the effect of very long investment horizons.

In the original Trinity Study, the quality of the conclusions was limited by the amount of historical data that was available. Because that study covered 71 years (1926–1995), there were really only three fully independent (nonoverlapping), complete, 20-year investment periods. There were only two 30-year investment periods. And there was only one 70-year period. We cannot, therefore, draw any useful inference about the performance of these asset classes over 70-year investment horizons, based on the historical data record alone. By modeling the behavior and interrelationships among various asset classes, however, we can produce a much richer data set and examine possibilities that would be unlikely to be observed in any particular, small set of historical observations.

The methodology I used to replicate and then extend the results of the Trinity Study is a Monte Carlo simulation based on *estimates* of steady-state long-run asset class returns, but using historical inflation and modern asset class volatilities and correlations based on the 1978–2012 period. I included headline inflation, nominal bonds, and equities.

Using this approach, I calculated a large number of hypothetical histories over different windows and calculated "portfolio success rates" to produce a table (Table 12.1) that is analogous to Table 3 in the Trinity Study, "Inflation-Adjusted Portfolio Success Rates: 1926 to 1995."

The estimates for steady-state returns are not drawn from the long-run historical returns ending in 1995, as they implicitly were in the Trinity Study, because using those returns biased success rates much higher since rising valuation levels over the historical period they used tended to overstate steady-state returns. Over their sample period, the arithmetic mean of equity market returns from 1925 to 1995 was 12.5 percent; the geometric mean was 10.5 percent. The compounded return *after inflation* was still a robust 7.2 percent. It is no surprise that equities look really good when held for the long run, especially if the long run starts in a period of low valuations and ends in a period of high valuations.

Unfortunately, this is not a reasonable return to expect from equities, especially when an aging demographic has lowered the potential growth rate of the developed world. In the next simulation (and all simulations thereafter), I assume that equities return 2 percent real growth, plus inflation, plus 2.5 percent dividend yield, for a 4.5 percent real yield. This is consistent with other modern work on the subject of expected equity returns.[6] You can refer to the original paper for the average return assumptions I use for inflation, inflation-indexed bonds, and nominal bonds, but remember that the Monte Carlo simulation allows them to fluctuate in each simulation run.

Note also that I am only using a subset of the universe of securities available to both individual and institutional investors. Later, I will discuss how "other assets" can be incorporated into the "easy" plan.

Table 12.1 is the first important and useful table in this chapter, but it only includes stocks and bonds so that you can easily see this point to be made about thrift: not surprisingly, the largest determinant of whether an investor's portfolio will survive over the long run is the withdrawal rate. This is a crucial point for investors with very long periods of retirement. If the investor insists on withdrawing 5 percent of the original portfolio, adjusted for inflation, each year, then no strategy involving stocks and bonds will provide him better than a 50–50 assurance of having any wealth left at the end of 30 years—and the numbers get worse the longer those withdrawals are taken.

Nominal bonds and equities are typical inclusions in this sort of exercise, but it is necessary to include TIPS (more generally, inflation-indexed bonds) because neither of those other two asset classes protects against inflation, the largest exposure for most retirees.

Therefore, in Tables 12.2 and 12.3 I expand the prior example to incorporate an asset class that was not included in the original Trinity Study (or in most other withdrawal rate studies): inflation-indexed bonds. To limit the size of the chart, I have chosen only two withdrawal rates, 4 percent and 5 percent. The 4 percent withdrawal rate is illustrated in Table 12.2; the 5 percent rate is in Table 12.3.

Each section of these two tables shows the proportion of the portfolio invested in TIPS at the top of the section, and then in the left-hand margin the amount invested in stocks (on the left) and bonds (on the right). For example, in Table 12.2, a portfolio of 20 percent TIPS, 40 percent stocks, and 40 percent bonds, over a 25-year investing period during which the investor takes a withdrawal every year of 4 percent of the original portfolio amount adjusted for inflation, would have a 91 percent success rate—meaning that in 91 percent of historical periods, we would expect the portfolio to last at least 25 years. I have put that number in **bold** type in the table, so you can see how the table is used to find that number.

TABLE 12.2   **Portfolio Success Rates: Monte Carlo Simulation (4% withdrawal rate)**

	Investing Horizon (years)				
Stocks/Bonds	15 yrs	20 yrs	25 yrs	30 yrs	35 yrs
TIPS Allocation: 0%					
100%/0%	96	87	78	68	59
75%/25%	99	93	83	72	62
50%/50%	100	96	88	75	59
25%/75%	100	98	89	74	56
0%/100%	100	96	79	58	39
TIPS Allocation: 20%					
80%/0%	99	92	82	72	63
60%/20%	100	97	88	75	66
40%/40%	100	98	**91**	78	63
20%/60%	100	100	92	77	57
0%/80%	100	98	83	60	39
TIPS Allocation: 40%					
60%/0%	100	97	89	77	65
45%/15%	100	99	92	80	68
30%/30%	100	100	96	81	64
15%/45%	100	100	95	77	53
0%/60%	100	99	89	67	41
TIPS Allocation: 60%					
40%/0%	100	100	94	82	66
30%/10%	100	100	96	82	64
20%/20%	100	100	98	83	61
10%/30%	100	100	97	79	52
0%/40%	100	100	93	68	42
TIPS Allocation: 80%					
20%/0%	100	100	98	87	62
15%/5%	100	100	98	83	57
10%/10%	100	100	98	82	51
5%/15%	100	100	97	77	45
0%/20%	100	100	94	71	39
All-TIPS Portfolio					
N/A	100	100	95	71	41

Note: Numbers rounded to the nearest whole percentage

TABLE 12.3 **Portfolio Success Rates: Monte Carlo Simulation (5% withdrawal rate)**

	Investing Horizon (years)				
Stocks/Bonds	15 yrs	20 yrs	25 yrs	30 yrs	35 yrs
TIPS Allocation: 0%					
100%/0%	88	71	60	48	42
75%/25%	94	79	62	49	39
50%/50%	98	84	63	44	33
25%/75%	99	85	57	34	22
0%/100%	97	75	43	22	12
TIPS Allocation: 20%					
80%/0%	93	79	63	50	40
60%/20%	97	82	63	48	35
40%/40%	99	89	63	42	28
20%/60%	100	88	56	30	16
0%/80%	99	78	46	22	8
TIPS Allocation: 40%					
60%/0%	98	87	65	49	36
45%/15%	100	88	66	43	29
30%/30%	100	92	65	36	20
15%/45%	100	90	54	24	11
0%/60%	100	84	44	18	6
TIPS Allocation: 60%					
40%/0%	100	90	66	42	27
30%/10%	100	93	64	35	19
20%/20%	100	95	61	26	11
10%/30%	100	94	55	19	6
0%/40%	100	88	42	15	4
TIPS Allocation: 80%					
20%/0%	100	96	63	26	9
15%/5%	100	95	58	20	6
10%/10%	100	96	54	17	4
5%/15%	100	94	47	15	3
0%/20%	100	91	44	12	3
All-TIPS Portfolio					
N/A	100	92	44	11	3

Note: Numbers rounded to the nearest whole percentage

The top sections of Tables 12.2 and 12.3, in which the allocation to TIPS is zero, corresponds to the relevant withdrawal column (either 4 percent or 5 percent) in Table 12.1 since in that first table we also did not include TIPS.

How to Use These Tables

If you are retired or nearing retirement, then using Tables 12.2 and 12.3 is fairly straightforward. First, choose a withdrawal rate with which you are comfortable. Again, the withdrawal rate is the percentage of the initial portfolio that you will withdraw every year, adjusted for inflation. As an example, if you have $500,000 in your portfolio and choose a 4 percent withdrawal rate, then in the first year you withdraw $20,000. In the second year, if inflation was 2 percent, you would withdraw $20,400 (which is $20,000 × 2%, plus the original $20,000). In the third year, you increase the $20,400 by the rate of inflation again, and so on. Note that the size of your withdrawals has nothing to do with the performance of your portfolio. This is, after all, supposed to be the easy way!

Once you have chosen your withdrawal rate, select a portfolio allocation from Table 12.2 (if you are using a 4 percent withdrawal rate) or Table 12.3 (if using 5 percent) where the column corresponds to the period of time you are assuming for your investment life. You will probably want to choose something with a high probability of success, but later I will explain why choosing the highest probability is not automatically the best choice.

If you are not retired, and so are still accumulating assets for your future retirement, then there are a couple of additional steps you need to take. First, you have to put yourself in the position of retirement and ask, "How much money would I need, per year, in today's dollars, to have the retirement I want?" For illustration, let us suppose that number is $80,000 per year.

From that, subtract what you expect to receive from other sources, such as Social Security. If you are expecting to get $30,000 per year from Social Security, it means you would need $50,000 per year, in today's dollars, to be provided from your investment accounts.

Now imagine that you are at retirement, and use Table 12.1 to select a withdrawal rate that provides you the minimum success rate you require for the length of requirement you expect to have. (We use Table 12.1 for this, peering into the dim future, because it is more conservative than Tables 12.2 and 12.3, and also because it gives more options for withdrawal rates.) If I expect a 25-year retirement, then Table 12.1 tells me I can withdraw 5 percent of the original balance per year, adjusted for inflation, and have an 89 percent chance of not running out of money if I invest 25 percent in stocks and 75 percent in bonds when I retire. Suppose that 89 percent is acceptable to me; I therefore decide a 5 percent future withdrawal rate suits me.

The next step is to *divide* the number of dollars you need per year by the withdrawal rate. In this example, $50,000 divided by 5 percent ($50,000/0.05) is $1 million. This means that when I retire, I have $1 million saved up and invest 25 percent in stocks and the rest in bonds, and I take $50,000 per year, adjusted for inflation, I expect to have an 89 percent chance of seeing that money last for at least 25 years.

Now that I know I need $1 million at retirement, I need to figure out how much I need to invest, per year, starting now, to have a good chance of reaching that goal. So we need an analogous table to Table 12.1: one that tells us what proportion of that goal I need to *save* every year, given the time remaining to retirement and the broad investment strategy I pursue. Table 12.4 provides that answer and works in similar fashion to Table 12.1. Figure out how long you have *until* retirement, and pick the portfolio allocation and contribution percentage that gives you the best chance of accumulating the nest egg you

TABLE 12.4   **Inflation-Adjusted Accumulation Success Rates: Monte Carlo Simulation**

Accumulation Period	Contribution Rate as a % of Targeted Terminal Portfolio Value:									
	3%	4%	5%	6%	7%	8%	9%	10%	11%	12%
100% Stocks										
10 Years	0	1	6	19	41	57	68	82	92	95
15 Years	13	32	54	72	86	92	96	98	99	99
20 Years	39	66	84	91	96	98	99	100	100	100
25 Years	66	85	94	98	99	100	100	100	100	100
75% Stocks/25% Bonds										
10 Years	0	0	2	13	33	60	77	87	94	98
15 Years	5	26	53	79	90	97	99	100	100	100
20 Years	34	67	90	96	99	100	100	100	100	100
25 Years	67	89	96	99	100	100	100	100	100	100
50% Stocks/50% Bonds										
10 Years	0	0	0	6	27	57	79	92	98	99
15 Years	1	15	50	81	95	99	100	100	100	100
20 Years	24	71	93	99	100	100	100	100	100	100
25 Years	69	93	99	100	100	100	100	100	100	100
25% Stocks/75% Bonds										
10 Years	0	0	0	1	15	48	82	96	100	100
15 Years	0	6	44	80	96	100	100	100	100	100
20 Years	13	66	94	99	100	100	100	100	100	100
25 Years	62	95	100	100	100	100	100	100	100	100
100% Bonds										
10 Years	0	0	0	1	13	43	72	91	98	100
15 Years	0	4	29	73	93	99	100	100	100	100
20 Years	11	54	87	99	100	100	100	100	100	100
25 Years	50	89	99	100	100	100	100	100	100	100

Note: Numbers rounded to the nearest whole percentage

have calculated. Continuing our example, if I have 25 years left until retirement, I find that I can achieve an 89 percent chance of accumulating that much money if I put aside 4 percent of it per year, and invest it 75 percent in equities and 25 percent in bonds.

Thus, if I save $40,000 per year, adjusted for inflation, for the next 25 years, and invest it 75/25 in stocks and bonds, I will very probably have at least $1 million in (inflation-adjusted) dollars, when I retire; I can then switch my allocation to 25/75 in stocks and bonds, and withdraw 5 percent per year for the next 25 years according to my plan.

Incidentally, you may wonder why saving $40,000 per year, adjusted for inflation, for 25 years does not guarantee that I will have $1 million in inflation-adjusted wealth at the end, since $40,000 times 25 equals $1 million exactly. The answer is revealing about the difference between real quantities and nominal quantities. If I save $40,000 per year, and bury it in the ground, then in 25 years I will in fact have $1 million *nominal* dollars. Money sitting idle is guaranteed a nominal return of zero. But neither stocks nor bonds are guaranteed a *real* return of zero, and, in fact, both have experienced considerable periods of sub-zero real returns historically. Thus, even if you sink $40,000 per year into stocks and bonds, and increase that amount every year for inflation, there is no guarantee that you will have $1 million in inflation-adjusted wealth in 25 years! (That being said, if you invested in inflation-linked bonds, you would have such certainty, as long as you were buying them when the current real yield was at least zero.)

Yes, folks, that is the *easy* method! Choosing a strategy in this way, using Tables 12.1 to 12.4, is designed to be, if not "fire-and-forget," at least "fire-and-course-correct." You should rebalance to your preferred weights periodically to take advantage of the third miracle of rebalancing. But there is no notion in these tables of "value." They are built on the basis of plausible long-run expected returns, variances, and covariances. There is also no notion of "momentum" in returns. Yet both value and momentum have been shown to potentially improve strategy returns over time, particularly when used in conjunction. What I would suggest for those investors who want an "easy-plus" plan is to use the method I've just discussed to allocate a large chunk of your assets—say, 80 percent—and then deploy any value or momentum strategies with the balance.

For example, perhaps you keep that last 20 percent in an equity-index fund when the S&P is above its 200-day moving average and in cash or a medium-term bond fund when it is below that average. This would be an example of a momentum strategy that you have overlaid on the primary "easy" strategy. Alternatively, you might use that approach with 10 percent and with the other 10 percent switch between bonds and inflation bonds in some way. But keep most of your assets, and the withdrawal or contribution rules, according to the previous tables.

Even better—call this "easy-plus-plus"—is to deploy those incremental assets in a low-cost systematic approach that incorporates notions of value as well as inflation awareness. As one example, I designed a strategy a few years ago that uses three simple rules to allocate between stocks, inflation-linked bonds, commodities, and cash. When real interest rates are high, it tends to hold stocks and TIPS; when real rates are low, it tends to hold commodities and cash, and so on. There are many such systems available.[7]

The overlay is also where asset classes other than stocks, bonds, and inflation-indexed bonds should go. Obviously, I couldn't put every asset class into these simple tables. If you want to have a commodities allocation, or invest in hedge funds, MLPs, and so on, put it in this "other" category.

Remember that the overall size of the overlay is up to you. Its size probably ought to be related to how much you have in your accounts, relative to what you require to fund your future. If you have barely enough to survive retirement, then the overlay should be a relatively small amount. But it could also be fairly large, if you are quite comfortable financially.

One final point: Inflation-aware investing is hard to do holistically if you do not have some knowledge of how various asset classes behave with respect to inflation. For example, if you want to increase equity exposure since you have heard that stocks are a hedge against inflation, it may surprise you to find out that stocks in general are a very *poor* hedge for inflation. I have developed a free email course that covers a number of asset classes; it may be interesting and/or helpful to readers who want to examine other asset classes in an inflation-aware context. You can sign up for the email course, which will drop an email to you every couple of days, at https://mikeashton .wordpress.com/free-inflation-investing-e-mail-seminar/.

Notes

1. Parts of this chapter, and chapter 13, borrow heavily from Michael Ashton, "Maximizing Personal Surplus: Liability-Driven Investment for Individuals," from *Retirement Security in the New Economy: Paradigm Shifts, New Approaches and Holistic Strategies*, Society of Actuaries, March 2011.
2. P. L. Cooley, C. M. Hubbard, and D. T. Walz, "Retirement Savings: Choosing a Withdrawal Rate That Is Sustainable," *American Association of Individual Investors Journal* 20 (2), (1998), pp. 16–21.
3. A withdrawal policy describes how the investor will draw on the portfolio over time. It is usually phrased as a proportion of the original portfolio value, and may be considered as either a level nominal dollar amount or adjusted for inflation (a real amount).
4. "Maximizing Personal Surplus: Liability-Driven Investment for Individuals," *op. cit.*

5. Michael Ashton, "Managing Laurels: Liability-Driven Investment for Professional Athletes," working paper, March 2013, available at http://papers.ssrn.com/sol3/papers.cfm?abstract_id=2408068.

6. See for example B. Cornell, and R. Arnott, *CRA Insights: Credit Crisis. The Basic Speed Law for Capital Markets Returns* (CRA International, 2008).

7. This particular strategy, which we call "Four-Real," is written up in a white paper and is freely available at http://www.enduringinvestments.com/papers/Four-Real-White-Paper.pdf.

CHAPTER 13

Liability-Driven Investing for Individuals

From the "easy" way, we move into a significantly more sophisticated way.

Institutions such as pension funds and endowments don't use the easy way to allocate assets. Perhaps some of the less sophisticated plans do, but over the last decade or two, another approach has gradually been adopted at these sorts of institutions—and, as it turns out, we can use the same approach to inform and improve the investing decision-making process of the individual investor.

In the "old way" of thinking about planning for retirement, the planning challenge consists of two questions as follows:

1. "How can I maximize return in the long run?"
2. "Given the riskiness of this portfolio, how do I set withdrawal policy to ensure I actually reach the long run?" with some trade-off of portfolio riskiness and withdrawal policy riskiness considered.

We saw a popular version of this approach in the prior chapter. A classic paper by William Bengen[1] in 1994 used historical data to determine that (in his opinion) the maximum safe withdrawal rate was 4 percent. In it, he writes:

Assuming a minimum requirement of 30 years of portfolio longevity, a first-year withdrawal of 4 percent, followed by inflation-adjusted withdrawals in subsequent years, should be safe. In no past case has it caused a portfolio to be exhausted before 33 years, and in most cases it will lead to portfolio lives of 50 years or longer.[2]

That was the origin of the now-famous *4 percent rule* that you may have heard of and that is still in general use as a rule-of-thumb for investors who want a *really* easy way. Lots of improvements have been made to this basic rule, such as the *ratcheting 4 percent rule* and the Trinity Study that I discussed (and improved upon) in the prior chapter. But for institutional investors such as pension funds, a much more fundamental insight has taken hold. These investors realize that planning for future expenditures such as pension fund payments or endowment gifts involves financing a relatively low-volatility stream of real and nominal expenses with a high-volatility stream of returns. For a pension fund, the liabilities are roughly fixed in real space and the assets are very volatile.

There is, in fact, a developing literature that concerns how to jointly consider both the asset mix and the spending requirement. That process is called liability-driven investing, or LDI.

What Is LDI?

The basic goal for these plans is to invest today in such a way as to ensure that future liabilities can be covered. The pension fund is not supposed to maximize its real assets, subject to risk constraints based on the variability of the asset portfolio; it is supposed to maximize the pension's economic *surplus*—the difference between its assets and liabilities—subject to constraints on the variability of the surplus.

The mandate to maximize economic surplus subject to its variability recognizes that the pension fund is not just a pool of assets but also a pool of liabilities that are to be funded with assets, and the mission of the plan sponsor is to consider these *together*.

To make this more concrete, let me suggest an example. Suppose you are saving for a child's college education in 18 years, and you can choose from three investments. The first investment is cash, and returns zero. The second investment is an ETF that tracks the broad stock market. The third investment is a fund that increases in value every year by an amount that tracks the increase in college tuitions.

Which of these three investments is the "best"? Well, on expected returns we would probably say that the stock market investment gives you the best expected return, over 18 years anyway. But is that the only relevant meaning of the word *best*? Which is the least *risky* choice? Would that be the cash investment?

No. As a matter of fact, the cash investment is highly risky in this context, because its performance is unrelated to the performance of the liability you are trying to match. Think of it like the problem of trying to hit with a tennis ball someone who is on a merry-go-round. If you are standing on the ground, this is not a trivial task if the merry-go-round is moving swiftly at all. But if you are also on the merry-go-round, then you are moving along with your target—and your chances of hitting that target go up considerably.

That is what "liability-driven investing" is all about: getting your assets on the same merry-go-round with your liabilities.

How LDI Is Applicable to Individuals

We must be careful to think about an individual investor's "liabilities" correctly. The liabilities of a pension or post-employment benefits fund are generally contractual or semi-contractual in nature. That is, there is a promise by the pension fund to pay a stream of future income to the beneficiary, or to

provide a stream of services of a certain type (as is the case
with a college's endowment, which is really in the business
of providing college education to future students). In the
individual's case, not all of the liabilities are contractual. Some,
of course, are: The home mortgage is a nominal liability with
known characteristics. So, too, are car payments, alimony
or child support payments, and other such things. But an
individual also has noncontractual liabilities that are no less
crucial to the planning exercise: "optional" fixed costs like life-
or long-term-care insurance premiums, as well as other costs
of living that tend to rise with inflation such as food, clothing,
utilities, entertainment, travel, and the like. Moreover, investors
may want to either explicitly fund a bequest or to treat part
of the portfolio as essentially carved out for the purpose, and
this may be nominal or real in nature. You, the investor, are
essentially running a very small pension fund for the benefit of
you, your family, and your heirs.

Of course, there are some important differences between a
pension fund's mandate and that of an individual investor. One
of the main ones has already been mentioned: the fact that
a pension fund generally has contractual terms that make its
liabilities relatively clear, while an individual investor generally
does not. A pension fund also benefits from actuarial averaging;
its exposure is to a *general* increase in longevity, for example,
or a spike in average medical costs. An individual, by contrast,
is exposed to the randomness of a single spin of the wheel of
fortune when it comes to his own longevity or the possibility
of large medical bills due to his own poor health.[3]

Why does the LDI mandate construction make sense in the
case of an individual as well as for a pension plan, endowment, or foundation? These investors have different merry-
go-rounds, but in each case the best plan is to *get on the right
merry-go-round* before you start flinging tennis balls. That
means that whether you are running a pension fund or your

retirement account, you should do so with an eye toward the relevant liabilities in your world.

Applying LDI in Your Planning

The rest of this section is necessarily general. The *complex* approach requires you to lay out a spreadsheet and model numbers far into the future. Only moderate financial knowledge is required to make a respectable stab at it, and the precise results will vary substantially based on your own personal circumstances. This chapter is only meant to give you some general guidelines for your work.

If you want to be liability-driven, the first thing you need to do is to figure out your liabilities! Make a list of all of the claims you have on future income. This can mean both classic liabilities, like a home mortgage, as well as commitments such as alimony, long-term care insurance premiums, and paying for college for children or grandchildren. It also needs to include the other kinds of spending you will do in the future, most of which can be thought of as generally rising with inflation. Also include future bequests, or the amount you want to leave to heirs. These are not all legal liabilities, but they are commitments that you have made, whether formally to others or informally to yourself, that represent future demands on your wealth.

You will need to determine whether these investments are *real,* meaning that their value will rise over time with inflation, or *nominal,* which means the dollar value of the liability is fixed. A mortgage is a nominal liability, at least in most places, while the cost of your future retirement is real (which is why we always talk in terms of *today's dollars,* even though we know your future cost of living will be higher).

You also need think about your illiquid assets that aren't part of your securities portfolio. Specifically, I am referring to things like your home and other real estate you may own. These items in particular have some inflation sensitivity to them; while they won't grow much faster than inflation, they will at least offset some of your needs for inflation-related investments.

And finally, you will need to think about how you feel about the upside and downside risks.

You Can't Take It with You

Stop the presses, but hear this: We have not yet figured out a way that you can take your extra wealth with you when you shuffle off this mortal coil.

What that means for the investing problem is that if your investing program produces too little money to finance your future liabilities, you are in bad shape. Depending on what your liabilities were, you may not be able to make that future bequest, or pay for your kids' education—or you might be eating $1 noodles and peanut butter and jelly and moving in with your kids during your retirement. On the other hand, while having great success with your investing program will make your life better, it does not help you in the afterlife if you die with lots of money saved up. In other words, the value of a "miss" when you take aim at your investment target is *asymmetric*. Consider Figure 13.1, which shows two different investment allocations, which, according to Table 12.2, have a 62 percent chance of lasting for 35 years for an investor with a 4 percent withdrawal rate. For each investment (initially worth $1,000 for the purposes of illustration), I have illustrated the median outcome at each annual date with a dotted line (where half of the outcomes of the Monte Carlo simulation are above, and half are below, the line), as well as the 5th percentile and the 95th percentile. One portfolio is 80 percent in TIPS and 20 percent in stocks and represented by thick, black lines; the other portfolio is 75 percent in stocks and 25 percent in regular (not inflation-linked) bonds and represented by thin, red lines.

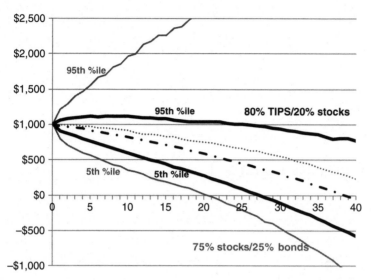

FIGURE 13.1 **Range of simulated outcomes for two strategies, 4 percent withdrawal rate**

Both of these investments may have a 62 percent chance of success for the investor, if "success" means that the money lasts until the 35th year. But notice the difference in the quality of the success. In the case of the equity/bonds mix, the investor stands a 5 percent chance of running out of money as soon as the 20th year: bankrupt, with 15 years left before the 35-year target time period is up! In the case of the TIPS-concentrated strategy, this unfortunate possibility doesn't enter at the 5 percent level until the 28th year of the simulation.

On the other hand, look at the upside! You would much rather own the upside of the equity and bonds portfolio. The question is, does the value of all that upside "balance" the risk of the downside? In finance theory, of course, it does. But does it represent balance for *you,* the person who would have to move in with the kids, if you get a bad draw from the markets? For that matter, what would the *kids* think of this trade-off? This is why higher "probabilities" of success are not necessarily automatically the right choice when presented with Tables 12.1, 12.2, or 12.3.[4]

The fancy way of making this observation is to say that the upside variance of the equity-concentrated mix does not "pay for" the downside variance, since those surpluses likely have considerably less salience to the 85-year-old investor than do the shortfalls. Scott, Sharpe, and Watson observed[5] that this is an inefficient use of investing dollars, and if the investor could sell some of that upside variance to buy downside protection, he likely should.

This is the decision that you, the investor, need to make because we can, to some degree, make that trade-off by altering the investment mix to better match assets and liabilities with each other and, as a result, reduce the variance of the net outcome. Table 13.1 shows that for the withdrawal rates illustrated in Tables 12.2 and 12.3, increasing concentrations of inflation-linked assets tend to increase the time to portfolio failure.

Applying the LDI Insight

When we depart from the realm of the theoretical, in which assets and liabilities are known, the investor only cares about portfolio exhaustion, and the portfolio is simple, we find that some complexity in the investment advisory process is warranted and can add value. We can then focus on choosing a portfolio that balances our desire to have a higher median outcome with long upper-tail possibilities and our desire to reduce the probability of portfolio failure. We see in Table 12.2 and Table 13.1 that high proportions of TIPS for reasonable withdrawal rates increase the time to 10 percent failure and decrease portfolio failure rates.

But suppose, instead, that we approached the problem by defining the true liability as the minimum amount of inflation-adjusted income we require for survival. Suppose you believe that a withdrawal of 3 percent of your current portfolio,

TABLE 13.1 Years to 10% Portfolio Failure Rate: Monte Carlo Simulation

	Withdrawal Rate	
Stocks/Bonds	4%	5%
TIPS Allocation: 0%		
100%/0%	19	15
75%725%	21	18
50%/50%	25	19
25%/75%	25	20
0%/100%	23	18
TIPS Allocation: 20%		
80%/0%	22	18
60%720%	25	19
40%/40%	27	20
20%/60%	27	21
0%/80%	25	19
TIPS Allocation: 40%		
60%/0%	25	19
45%/15%	27	20
30%730%	28	21
15%/45%	28	22
0%/60%	26	20
TIPS Allocation: 60%		
40%/0%	28	22
30%/10%	29	22
20%720%	29	22
10%730%	29	22
0%/40%	26	21
TIPS Allocation: 80%		
20%/0%	30	22
15%15%	30	23
10%/10%	29	22
5%/15%	28	22
0%/20%	27	22
All-TIPS Portfolio		
N/A	27	21

Note: Numbers rounded to the nearest whole percentage

adjusted for inflation, would be sufficient to provide a low, but satisfactory, standard of living in a worst-case scenario for your expected 30-year retirement period. At a 2 percent expected long-term real return on TIPS, this means that approximately 67 percent of the portfolio should be allocated to TIPS to reduce the probability of portfolio failure to a negligible level. The 67 percent figure is the present value of a real amount of 3 percent received annually for 30 years, discounted at a 2 percent real rate, and can be calculated in Excel as PV (2%, 30, 3%). This is what a person would pay, before fees, for an inflation-adjusted annuity if they were available. They generally are *not* available, but you could accomplish essentially the same thing by buying actual TIPS (not a fund) that had a 2 percent real yield.

Here is where the LDI insight—the recognition of the dynamic nature of the investor's liability exposure, relative to his assets—comes into play. Recall that in Figure 13.1, the high-TIPS strategy bought security at the cost of losing a fair amount of the "upside tail" outcomes. This is because the strategy did not adapt to the changing circumstances of the investor, with respect to his assets and liability mix over time. When the portfolio experienced "good outcomes," it responded by allocating the profits 80 percent into TIPS and 20 percent into stocks. When the portfolio experienced "bad outcomes," it responded by liquidating the portfolio in the same proportion.

But that approach ignores the fact that good portfolio returns (and/or a declining retirement "liability" as the retiree ages) can be allocated to risky investments without threatening the retiree's security—which is covered by the "liability-immunizing portfolio" (TIPS in this case)—while bad portfolio returns should first be covered by liquidating the risky securities, rather than lessening the degree of protection that the retiree has. One can think about the overall portfolio being split into a *liability-immunizing* account and a *risk-seeking*

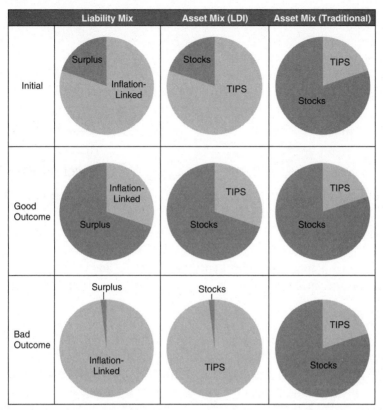

FIGURE 13.2 **The LDI asset mix seeks to match the liabilities' characteristics.**
Source: Hypothetical illustration

account and get the general idea. Figure 13.2 illustrates the difference between the traditional "best portfolio" approach and the LDI approach, in which inflation-linked liabilities are matched with inflation-linked assets and the free surplus is matched with "return-seeking" strategies.

The result of taking the liability-driven approach is to preserve more of the value of the upside tails, while truncating the downside tails. Figure 13.3 illustrates the range of simulation outcomes for a withdrawal rate of 3 percent. As before, the dotted line indicates the median portfolio outcome while the top

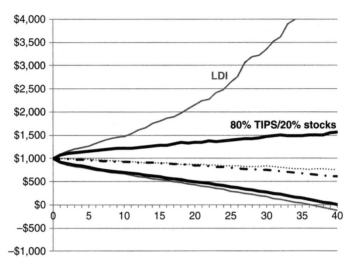

FIGURE 13.3 **Range of simulated outcomes for static and LDI strategies, 3 percent withdrawal rate**

line is the 95th percentile and the bottom line is the 5th percentile. In one case (shown in thick, black lines), the investor allocates 80 percent to TIPS and 20 percent to stocks in a static portfolio allocation (i.e., "Traditional," in Figure 13.2). In the other case (shown in thin, red lines), the investor initially has 80 percent in TIPS and 20 percent in stocks, but then changes that allocation annually based on the overall portfolio value and the value of the remaining *security liability*. Occasionally, this means that after a run of bad luck, the investor ends up holding a portfolio that is entirely in TIPS, but sometimes after a run of good luck, especially as the investor ages and has a shorter "security" horizon, the investor is heavily into equities—but in this case, as opposed to the earlier cases we saw, without risking complete portfolio failure.

There is no question here which portfolio will be preferred by an investor.

For investors who can just barely fund the security portfolio while taking out the bare minimum withdrawal, LDI will have less salience. Such an investor starts with a very small margin of safety, and is unlikely to parlay that into a big risk-seeking portfolio. But for an investor with sufficient assets that the security portfolio can be fully funded with less than 90 percent of the total asset base, this is a powerful approach that improves the investor's security while still giving many opportunities to realize an "upside tail."

In summary, the LDI method boils down to these steps, simplified so that you don't need to run Monte Carlo simulations if you want to do it yourself:

1. Compute the amount of real liabilities and nominal liabilities you have, and the present values of future real and nominal cash flows (such as a mortgage) you are obliged to pay. You should also include in your list of liabilities the present value of the *minimum* cost of the standard of living you can accept in retirement.

2. Compute the amount of real assets and nominal assets you have, excluding your securities portfolio and the present values of future real and nominal cash flows (such as Social Security) you are entitled to receive.

3. Figure out the net real asset or liability and the net nominal asset or liability; figure out the length of the period over which the securities portfolio assets will need to meet those liabilities. Then back into the size of your rainy-day portfolio using the Excel function PV (real interest rate, number of years, dollars needed per year). For real expenses, use a reasonable long-term real interest rate like 2 percent; for nominal expenses, use a reasonable long-term nominal interest rate like 4 or 5 percent.

4. The sum of these two numbers is your rainy-day fund, the minimum you need to meet your liabilities. Typically, the part of the rainy-day fund that is to meet nominal liabilities would be invested in Treasuries, while the part of

the rainy-day fund that is to meet real liabilities would be invested in TIPS.

5. Any surplus over that amount may be invested in "risky" securities, with the idea that even a bad loss will not impact your ability to meet your future liabilities. From time to time, if you wish, reallocate some of the gains into your "rainy day" portfolio to ratchet up the floor value of your future retirement quality.

Congratulations. You are now a pension fund manager for a pension of one!

Notes

1. W. P.,Bengen, "Determining Withdrawal Rates Using Historical Data," *Journal of Financial Planning* 7 (4), 171–180.
2. Ibid.
3. And this is why individuals should have health insurance that covers disasters, and why life annuities that last forever—in case you also last forever—are worth considering in just about any plan.
4. It is also the reason that *lower* probabilities of success are not necessarily the *wrong* choice in Table 12.4. The upside matters a lot more in the accumulation phase, because you will get to use that upside in retirement!
5. J. S. Scott, W. F. Sharpe, and J. G. Watson, "The 4% Rule—At What Price?" *Journal of Investment Management* (Third Quarter 2009), available at SSRN: http://ssrn.com/abstract=1115023.

CHAPTER 14

Investing for a Currency Calamity

Imagine a time in the near or distant future. A president stands at the window, despondent. An order sits on the Presidential desk, awaiting a signature, while the Cabinet waits respectfully. The order would nationalize the banks and seize a significant portion of depositors' assets. A separate order, arranged neatly beneath the first order, would "redenominate" the currency by declaring one of the new money units to be worth one million of the old unit. Practically speaking, this will be effected by striking out the last six zeroes on the existing banknotes.

"How did it come to this?" murmurs the President. The people in the room shift uncomfortably, staring at their shoes. "Only three years ago, inflation was 4 percent. Two years ago, it was 40 percent. Last year it was 400 percent. And now?" The labor secretary responds to the glance and begins to stammer a reply. "It doesn't matter," interrupts the President. "No one uses money anyway."

It was true, and they all knew it. Tax collections had converged on zero, because commerce was no longer conducted with money. This had happened fairly suddenly, around the time that inflation had lurched right off the charts in the daily briefing books. They all remembered how they had learned of the rise of the barter economy: The Secretary of Education had told them that the teachers' union was publishing recommended barter prices for teachers, along with an instructional narrative—part of which the Secretary had read to them: "Terry, who teaches high school literature, would use Table A to figure out how to collect his salary, depending on what goods were available to the school. If he also coached the cross-country team, he should add the ancillary values in Table A(2). The values are given in terms of Universal Labor Units (ULUs), to facilitate comparison with hypothetical prices of goods and services in ULU—shown on Table C..."

No one knew what a Universal Labor Unit was worth, in terms of currency, because the teachers' union had invented the ULU. The National Firearms Brotherhood pursued a similar approach, listing informatively for its members the latest exchange rates between certain goods and ammunition of various types. On the NFB website, the group argued that ammunition made an excellent medium of exchange because of its inherent usefulness and its easy divisibility, and scoffed at the "squishy ULU concept introduced by the Socialists."

What a mess. The President had tried wage and price controls, but that had merely given the black market a head start. And now that the sovereign currency was no longer accepted, the whole notion of fixed prices made no sense. Fixed relative to what? In terms of the number of bullets a good carpenter could earn in a day, prices were already reasonably stable—if you could figure out what they were in the first place...

"Ahem." The defense secretary cleared her throat, calling them all back from their reminiscences. "On the matter we all came here to discuss. How do we plan to pay the soldiers? Our southern border is already hard-pressed, and our soldiers are starting to desert. We are not taking in any taxes, we cannot borrow money, enlisted men refuse to take fresh printed currency that no one else will honor, and the soldiers don't seem to relish the idea of possibly taking a bullet for an IOU that our country might not be around to honor."

"What?" The President looked up sharply, seemingly energized for the first time since the meeting had begun. "We will overcome this. We are strong. We are a nuclear power!"

The defense Secretary shrugged. "Are we going to shoot off nukes on our own border? We need manpower, and equipment. Speaking of which: How can I get more fuel for our tanks? Do you know anyone who will trade us gasoline for a one-megaton nuclear weapon?"

"I do," said the Secretary of State. "But you're not gonna like it."

* * *

Up to this point in this book, I have addressed the possibility, and even the probability, of the return of what I would call "uncomfortable" levels of inflation due to lazy and/or incompetent central banking. In Chapter 5, I proposed that fiat money fails slowly, suddenly, or slowly and *then* suddenly. In this vignette, the country's money fails slowly, but at an accelerating pace, until faith in the money collapses altogether, and all at once.

Perhaps this scene is far-fetched; perhaps not. The question I want to address, though, is this: If such a case is what you fear, how should you invest? I am not terribly worried yet about such an outcome, but when we invest we consider potentialities because the future is unknown. If the collapse of the financial system, of money itself, is a possibility, how should you invest? What should you do to hedge the possibility that fiat money becomes worthless?

Is Gold a Disaster Hedge?

A popular answer has long been "hold gold," but I have to tell you that this is not a satisfying answer. In ages past, holding gold was helpful because of its dense value (a single pound is worth on the order of $20,000 today) and because many countries' currencies were convertible into gold. The latter point is, sadly, no longer true.

This means that someone who holds a significant part of his (her) wealth in gold cannot automatically trade it at some predefined exchange rate. In a calamity, perhaps everyone will suddenly accept gold coins in exchange for goods and services. But I cannot think of why they would. Gold is not inherently valuable to me. I cannot eat it or use it. I can wear it, but I suspect post-Armageddon bling has limited utility. If other people hold the same view as I do, then why would I take your gold coin? It is no more exchangeable than a pile of cigarettes or ammunition or cans of soup. Because of its density, it is more storable, but it is also less divisible—and less useful.

I recognize that many people feel strongly about gold as a hedge against inflation. These people often also feel strongly about gold as a hedge against deflation. I am not going to persuade many of these people that they shouldn't hold gold, but then again I am not trying to do so. There is nothing wrong with gold. But there is also nothing special about gold, compared to any other dense, storable commodity. If I build a fence for you and you offer to pay me in Krugerrands—but I am unable to trade Krugerrands for a type of currency that I know to be generally accepted—then how many Krugerrands should I ask for? Like any other potential money stand-in, I have to know what the exchange rate is between this item and any others I wish to buy. This is no different from trading in cigarettes, except that I have a much better sense with the latter what its value in use is, and therefore what the floor on its value ought to be.

This is not to say that gold is not a worthwhile investment; merely that it is not a *unique* investment.

Real Property

Gold is just one form of real property. Along with real estate, ammunition, silver, copper, coffee, sugar, rice, diamonds, or cattle (and we could name many others!). Some of these are more storable than others; some are more portable than others. Both of those qualities are very useful, which is one reason that people gravitate towards precious metals. Real estate tends to hold its value better (Will Rogers said that's because God isn't making any more of it) and to have more moderate swings in value than do the precious metals; however, real estate is utterly immobile. What that means is that in an economic collapse, it can be seized. Of course, so can the other types of real property, but they can also be hidden.

Precious metals or precious gems may offer the best combination of storability and portability (and hide-ability!). But when it comes to real assets, I don't want all of my eggs in one basket until I know what the preferred basket will be. Gold, silver, diamonds, real estate, wine, and classic cars: give me *options*.

If you are actually worried about financial catastrophe, incidentally, hold the physical stuff rather than trust receipts. I personally don't worry about holding gold bullion in preference to the GLD exchange-traded fund, but if there is a true catastrophe like the one illustrated to start this chapter, the pieces of paper you own will be of little help in trade.

Human Capital

The ultimate in portability is to have nothing to carry. Medical doctors will always have something to barter, as will electricians, carpenters, and anyone hale and hearty enough, and not too proud, to chop wood or dig a ditch. Authors and bloggers? Not so much.

If you are worried about the ultimate collapse, invest in human capital. Keep yourself fit; study, and keep learning new skills.

Invest in family. Invest in your support network. Prepare for the lean years by laying up stores of favors with friends. Be generous with your time and talents, and your network may help you if there is ever a need. I don't understand people who prepare for an apocalyptic future by becoming hermits.[1]

A hermit need support only himself, but has no one to rely on for help or to divide labor. Remember from Chapter 1 that even in a barter economy, there are gains to specialization and trade.

Invest in the present, and in making that present a memorable past. Happy memories and hopes for the future can sustain you when the world falls apart around you. The worst financial catastrophes of the past did not persist indefinitely. Better days are always ahead, eventually, and to survive until you get to those better days it helps to have someone to hug.

You can hug gold, but it won't hug you back.

Note

1. That is, unless it involves zombies. Then I totally understand being a hermit.

Index